Contents

D0206681

7 Acknowledgments

9 Introduction

19 STAGE 1 : STARTING OFF RIGHT

20 Tips for Leading Name Games

21 Name Games

21 Singing Names

22 Names in Action

22 Slap, Clap, Snap!

23 Toss-a-Name

24 It's Your Birthday

24 Name Pulse

25 Silent Scramble

25 Bumpity, Bump Bump Bump!

26 Name Games Plus

26 Behind Every Name

27 The Name Game

28 Milling to Music

29 Share and Tell

30 That's Me!

31 Team Banners

32 Sticky IDs

33 Crossword Connections

34 Beyond Names: Getting to *Really* Know You!

34 The Matching Game

35 Take a Hike

36 In the Spotlight

37 Four on a Couch

38 Peek-a-Who?

38 License Plates

39 Mystery Partners

41 STAGE 2 : BUILDING RELATIONSHIPS

42 Tips for Leading Relationship-Building Games

43 Fun Warm-Ups

43 Zip Bong

43 Zoom

44 Who's the Leader?

45 You're a Star!

46 Leadership Line-Up

47 Hog Call

48 You Belong!

48 Impulse

49 Mini-Scavenger Hunt

50 The Smiling Game

52 Personality Plus

52 Colorful Conversations

54 Animal Corners

54 Personality Sketches

56 Conversation Starters

56 Bag of Questions

57 Pan Game

57 Family Chatter

58 Ticket Talk

59 Two Truths and a Lie

60 Diversity Appreciation

60 Common Ground

61 Tiny Teach

62 Diversegories

64 Diversity ABCs

65 Human Treasure Hunt

67 Energy Builders

67 Bounce

67 Sit Down, Stand Up

68 Finger Fencing

68 One-Handed Shoe Tie

68 Talking Points

69 Signal Switch

69 Life Story

70 National Air Guitar Competition

70 Dance Craze

71 Airplane Aerobics

73 STAGE 3 : BECOMING A TEAM

73 Tips for Leading Team-Building Games

75 Physical Warm-Ups

75 Funny Bones

75 Player to Player

77 Four Corners Dash

78 Physical Challenges

78 Raise the Bar

79 Jungle Beat

80 Last One Standing

81 Shrinking Ship

82 Pass the Can

83 Tag Games

83 Predators and Prey in the City

84 Cat and Dog Chase

84 Going for "It"

85 Blob Tag

86 "It" Tag

87 Elbow Tag

88 Relays

88 Airplane Relay

89 Over and Under

90 Speed Rabbit

91 On Your Mark

92 Having a Ball

92 Diversity Toss

93 Group Juggle

94 Zip!

96 Precious Treasure

97 Popcorn

98 Elevation

99 Balloon Games

99 Balloon Bop

99 Balloon Body Bop

100 Balloon Body Combo Bop

100 Balloon Chaos

101 Fire in the Hole

102 Scavenger Hunts

102 Quick Scavenger Hunt

104 Digital Scavenger Hunt

106 Word Games

106 Spell Off

107 Four Letter Words!

108 20 Words or Less

109 Alphabet Race

110 Parallel Words

111 Group Collaborations

111 Story Circles

112 Group Poetry

GREAT GROUP GAMES

175 Boredom-Busting,
Zero-Prep Team Builders for All Ages

SUSAN RAGSDALE and **ANN SAYLOR**

SEARCH
INSTITUTE
PRESS

Great Group Games:
175 Boredom-Busting, Zero-Prep
Team Builders for All Ages

The following are registered
trademarks of Search Institute:
Search Institute®,
Developmental Assets®,

and **HEALTHY YOUTH**®

Susan Ragsdale and Ann Saylor

Search Institute Press
Copyright © 2007 by Search Institute

All rights reserved. No parts of this publication
may be reproduced in any manner, mechanical
or electronic, without prior permission from the
publisher except in brief quotations or sum-
maries in articles or reviews, or as individual
activity sheets for educational use only. For
additional permission, write to Permissions at
Search Institute.

The content of this book has been reviewed
by a number of youth leadership and youth
development professionals. Every effort has
been made to provide sound direction for each
game described herein. The authors, publisher,
and reviewers take no responsibility for the use
or misuse of any materials or methods described
in this book, and will not be held liable for any
injuries caused by playing games from this
book. Please use prudent judgment and take
appropriate safety precautions when playing
all games.

10
Printed on acid-free paper in the United States
of America.

Search Institute
615 First Avenue Northeast, Suite 125
Minneapolis, MN 55413
www.search-institute.org
612-376-8955 • 877-240-7251

ISBN-13: 978-1-57482-196-3
ISBN-10: 1-57482-196-2

Credits
Editors: Anitra Budd, Susan Wootten
Cover Design: Percolator
Interior Design: Jeenee Lee
Production Coordinator: Mary Ellen Buscher

Library of Congress
Cataloging-in-Publication Data

Ragsdale, Susan.
    Great group games : 175 boredom-busting,
zero-prep team builders for all ages / Susan
Ragsdale & Ann Saylor.
    p. cm.
    Summary: "This resource, for all ages, offers a wide
range of activity choices: icebreakers, "straight-
up" games, and reflection activities, perfect for
classrooms, after-school programs, retreats,
workshops, and groups on the go. The fun games
and activities will have participants engaged and
involved, making every moment meaningful"--
Provided by publisher.
    Includes bibliographical references and index.
    ISBN-13: 978-1-57482-196-3
      (pbk. : alk. paper)
    ISBN-10: 1-57482-196-2 (pbk. : alk. paper)
1. Group games. I. Saylor, Ann. II. Title.

GV1203.R335 2007
790.1'5--dc22
                                    2007002560

"Fire in the Hole" and "Add it Up" (called "Diversegories" in this book) are adapted with permission
of Kendall/Hunt Publishing from Youth Leadership
in Action by Project Adventure.

About Search Institute Press
Search Institute Press is a division of Search
Institute, a nonprofit organization that offers
leadership, knowledge, and resources to promote
positive youth development. Our mission at
Search Institute Press is to provide practical and
hope-filled resources to help create a world in
which all young people thrive. Our products are
embedded in research, and the 40 Developmental
Assets®—qualities, experiences, and relationships
youth need to succeed—are a central focus of our
resources. Our logo, the SIP flower, is a symbol
of the thriving and healthy growth young people
experience when they have an abundance of assets
in their lives.

113 TV Remixes

113 Name That Tune

114 Expert Reviewers

114 Unfair Quiz Show

116 TV Families

117 By the Board

117 Trivia Masters

118 Trivia Acts

119 Picture Perfect

120 Clay Artists

121 Create-a-Game

122 The Big Issues Board Game

123 Building Blockbusters

124 Scatter Categories

125 Creative Pursuits

125 Build a Boat

126 Human Machines

127 Nature Sculptures

128 Clay Sculptures

129 Kitchen Creations

130 Card Castles

131 Lights, Camera, Action!

131 Song Off

132 Bag of Skits

133 Create a Message

134 Commercial Spots

135 Pantomime Pairs

136 The Artist

136 Artist of the Day

136 Blind Design

137 Who Am I?

139 Back-to-Back Art

141 STAGE 4 : DEEPENING TRUST

142 Tips for Leading Trust Games

143 Express Yourself

143 Take a Stand

144 What Would You Do If . . . ?

146 Debate a View

147 Values Continuum

149 Two Circles

151 Life Lines

152 Crossing the Line

154 Last Detail

155 Wink, Wink!

156 Sticky Buns

158 Tips for Leading Safe Trust-Leaning Activities

162 Trust Leans

162 Backward Lean

163 Forward Lean

164 Leaning Book Ends

165 Compass Lean

166 Wind in the Willows

167 Trust Lift

168 Trust Walk

169 Trust Fall

170 Bounce Machine

171 Tandem Stand Up

172 Sherpa Walk

173 STAGE 5 : CHALLENGING THE TEAM

174 **Tips for Leading Problem-Solving Initiative Games**

175 **Initiatives and Puzzlers**

175 Magical Stones

178 Blind Count

179 Ice Cream Sundae Challenge

180 Snowshoes

181 Change Over

181 All Aboard

182 The Chocolate Factory

184 Guiding Lights

185 The Winding Road

187 The Winding Road: Crossing the Pit of Despair

188 The Winding Road: Crossing the Sea of Hope

190 Perfect Square

191 Mission Possible

192 Two-Sided Toss

194 Hidden Hands

195 STAGE 6 : AFFIRMING CHANGES AND CELEBRATING SUCCESSES

196 **Tips for Leading Transition and Celebration Games**

197 **Ideas for Celebrations and Transitions**

198 **Just for Laughs!**

198 Hula Hoop Challenge

199 Ha! Ha!

200 The Ahhh! Game

200 Balloon Launch

201 Coin Toss Relay

202 Puzzle Relay

204 **On a Positive Note**

204 Positive Vibes Jam

205 Pats on the Back

205 Musical Chairs Affirmations

206 Mail Carriers

207 Personal Keys Puzzle

208 **On a Thoughtful Note**

208 Music Makers

209 Grab Bag

210 Talent Web

211 Snapshots

211 Opposite Ends

213 **On a Ceremonial Note**

213 Box of Life

214 Talking Stick

215 APPENDIXES

216 **It's All in the Questions**

219 **Game Index**

225 **Game Sources**

Acknowledgments

Play is vital to our lives—essential for the soul, for laughter, for building relationships, and for learning. Play helps us keep sane, make sense of our lives, and enjoy a seemingly mad world. And it's just plain *fun*. This book evolved from our years of play—as goofy kids (and adults) who couldn't let go of a good time; as game participants, camp counselors, and teen workers in church and school settings; and as professional youth trainers at the YMCA and other youth-serving organizations.

Early in our careers, we discovered the games of Karl Rohnke, the "godfather" of all games book authors. His book, *Silver Bullets* (Dubuque, IA: Kendall/Hunt Publishing Co., 1989), helped us grow groups into teams through adventure games and trust initiatives. We'd be remiss if we didn't tip our hats in Karl's direction; we note in particular games that nurtured creative inspiration in our work: "Booop," "Everybody's It," "BRAAAAAAACK-WHFFFFF," and "Basic Killer." We also thank Mary Hohenstein, who compiled *A Compact Encyclopedia of Games, Games, Games for People of All Ages* (Minneapolis, MN: Bethany House Publishers, 1980). We found golden nuggets in her book, including "High Water—Low Water" and "Hunker Hawser," that sparked creative insights and led to freshness and creativity as we took games to a deeper level.

Besides these games experts, we send a big, old-fashioned Southern *thank you* to our friends and colleagues who have influenced how we view and do our work (game masters in their own right, every last one of them). Special thanks to the following folks for sharing favorite games and giving us feedback: Spencer Bonnie, Jennifer Gilligan Cole, Justin Crowe, Jennifer Fauss, Greg Glover, David Kelly-Hedrick, Laura Meverden, Nicole Modeen, Tommy Royston, Cynthia Scherer, Nancy Short, Henry Smith, Mark Thomas, Bill Van de Griek, Sharon Williams, and Ellen Zinkiewicz. Thanks for being our playmates and teaching us so much.

Thank you to editor Tenessa Gemelke at Search Institute for first seeing the spark within and demanding that we follow it, and to Anitra Budd and Susan Wootten for shepherding us through the writing process and making it ever so easy. And we can't forget Peter Benson—thanks for saying "yes!"

And—saving the best for last—a final thanks to our husbands, Pete and Dan, who bounced around our ideas and provided us with feedback, encouragement, and understanding. Thanks for putting up with us!

SUSAN RAGSDALE & ANN SAYLOR

Introduction

This book is about games—*fun* games. But it's even more than that. Games are a great tool for creating teachable moments while players younger and older have a good time. Need something to break the ice? Get everyone back on track? Build trust and cooperation? Take your group to the next level of development? If you answered "yes" to any of these questions, then this book is a must.

Having a few games up your sleeve for a rainy or even an ordinary day is a no-brainer for any youth worker, camp counselor, group leader, orientation advisor, trainer, presenter, or teacher. In *Great Group Games: 175 Boredom-Busting, Zero-Prep Team Builders for All Ages,* you'll find an easy-to-use book of games to satisfy your most demanding critics and keep them laughing and learning. These games offer an opportunity to "play with a purpose."

As you delve into the book, you may find some of the games seem familiar, although not quite the way you've processed them before. What's *new* is playing the games in a way that will help your group develop broader skills, stronger confidence, and meaningful, supportive relationships. With a little tweak here and there, a change of a rule or a new step or two, and accompanied by stimulating reflection questions, each game ties in to Search Institute's research-based Developmental Assets® framework—the 40 qualities, values, and experiences youth need to succeed and grow into healthy, caring, competent individuals (see "Developmental Asset Categories" on page 10).

Varied and entertaining, these games can help groups of youth and adults from 12 to 112 get off to a great start, build relationships, transform the group into a team, deepen trust among group members, solve problems, overcome challenges, and celebrate successes. All the games in this book can be played by youth and adults together, emphasizing the importance of intergenerational partnerships. Cooperative games can put youth and adults on an equal footing and demonstrate that each has something to offer and teach the other. These games are designed to help players feel safe, welcome, included, and valued, as well as make friends, build skills and self-esteem, develop confidence, and gain a sense of personal power. Players can explore their creative, intellectual, and physical sides and discover special gifts in the process.

So roll up your sleeves and have fun goofing around with everyone in your group. When you lead groups through various games,
you'll find what happens is part magic, part insight, and part wisdom.
The magic comes from what can happen in the group as individuals
blossom and the group grows together. As you learn to "read" your
group, you can provide insight for them and adjust games and team
building according to what's working and what's not. Reading the
group is hard work and takes experience and time. The good news
is that you can keep in mind certain patterns in the way groups work
to avoid some of the pitfalls of leading groups and playing with
each other.

Benefits of Playing Games

Play is a natural part of growth and development. In early childhood
and elementary school, play is essential to healthy social, emotional,
and physical development. As children grow older (and for adults,
too), play provides continued health benefits, allowing breaks from
the tensions and difficulties of life. Play refreshes and invests spirits
with exuberance and vigor, and renews creativity and energy for

DEVELOPMENTAL ASSET CATEGORIES

Search Institute's extensive research
has identified 40 Developmental
Assets®, the critical building blocks
of healthy youth development. Assets
are organized into the following eight
asset categories:

Support—Young people need
to be surrounded by people
who love, care for, appreciate, and
accept them.

Empowerment—Young people
need to feel valued and valuable. This happens when young
people feel safe and respected.

Boundaries and Expectations—
Young people need clear rules,
consistent consequences for breaking
rules, and encouragement to do
their best.

problem solving, clarity, and fresh insights. Playing games also provides the following benefits:

- Levels the playing field and invites participants to interact with one another.

- Helps participants get comfortable with a group, ease anxieties, and form relationships with new people.

- Involves multiple aspects of participants' personalities and minds, by engaging them verbally, intellectually, creatively, and physically.

- Create teachable moments and offer a safe venue to recognize and talk about behaviors that are often difficult to discuss directly in real-world situations.

- Allows participants to practice new behaviors (such as better communication, assertiveness, cooperation, and problem-solving) before trying them in real-world activities with real-life consequences.

- Brings closure to group activities through reflection, affirmation, and celebration.

Constructive Use of Time— Young people need opportunities—outside of school—to learn and develop new skills and interests with other youth and adults.

Commitment to Learning— Young people need a sense of the lasting importance of learning and a belief in their own abilities.

Positive Values—Young people need to develop strong guiding values or principles to help them make healthy life choices.

Social Competencies— Young people need the skills to interact effectively with others, to make difficult decisions, and to cope with new situations.

Positive Identity—Young people need to believe in their own self-worth and to feel that they have control over the things that happen to them.

To download a complete list of Search Institute's Developmental Assets in English and Spanish, visit search-institute.org/assets/assetlists.html

How to Use This Book

We've organized this book in a way that highlights stages of group development:

- **STAGE 1: STARTING OFF RIGHT**
  Every group has a beginning, and beginnings continue whenever new people join the group. These games establish connections, create a safe environment, ensure everyone is included, and provide opportunities to get to know each other in fun ways.

- **STAGE 2: BUILDING RELATIONSHIPS**
  Building relationships is an ongoing process. This section offers a variety of games to help keep relationships positive and enjoyable. They include activities that you can do repeatedly to energize and engage a group.

- **STAGE 3: BECOMING A TEAM**
  Games in this section help a group form an identity as a team. A wide variety of game types (physical, verbal, dramatic, and creative) provide opportunities for players to express, appreciate, and complement individual skills, as well as learn to cooperate and work together.

- **STAGE 4: DEEPENING TRUST**
  Trust games take the team to a higher level of growth and development, both physically and emotionally. These games encourage players to expand their comfort zones without dampening their spirits, and allow players to express and clarify their opinions.

- **STAGE 5: CHALLENGING THE TEAM**
  Problem-solving "initiative" games propel the team into scenarios that enable participants to tackle particular risks and puzzles, develop leadership skills, and resolve conflicts.

- **STAGE 6:**
  AFFIRMING CHANGES AND CELEBRATING SUCCESSES
  Games enable reflection on changes and transitions. They also reinforce positive identity, celebrate talents and successes, and emphasize group learning and growth. These games are

important and useful in marking the end of a meeting or program and for providing transitions in the group (greeting new members or saying goodbye) for rites of passage, and upon completion of projects.

Each game stage begins with an explanation and contains game-specific tips. The games in each section are designed for the specific stage of team building and are grouped by game type. The format for each game is: *Title, Time* (estimated range), *Supplies, Set Up* (as needed), *Note* or *Safety Note* (as needed), *The Game* (instructions, rules, and any particular recommendations about group size), *Variations* (for some games), *Going Deeper* (reflection questions), and *Asset Categories* links. Most games require little to no preparation, but occasionally some advance set up is advised. Reflection questions allow groups to discuss and process what happened while playing the game, as well as address specific Developmental Assets.

In "Appendixes" (see page 219) you'll find a helpful Game Index that notes *Location* for games (indoors or outdoors), *Risk Level* (low, medium, or high), *Energy Level* (calm and sitting to active and moving), and whether nominal *Supplies* are needed. You'll also find "It's All in the Questions," (see page 216), a series of conversation openers that can be used with many of the games. Use the Game Leader Notes (see page 227) to add your favorite games and to write additional discussion questions.

Tips for Game Leaders

To make sure game time passes smoothly, be sure to tailor every game to your specific group's style and needs. You can easily adapt most games in this book to suit people of varied abilities and skill levels, but you might need to be creative with your resources and space. Consider any and all limitations as you schedule and plan games. Here are some questions you'll need to ask yourself:

Who's Playing?

ABILITIES The physical and mental development of individuals in the group will greatly affect the game's outcome. Consider everyone's potential participation. Are participants:

- Coordinated and strong enough to handle any physical challenges?

- Intellectually able to problem-solve at the game's degree of difficulty?

- Old enough to appreciate and learn from the issues the game raises?

- Able to use their natural learning styles with the games you've chosen?

- In need of adaptations that will help them be successful (e.g., visual prompts for games that involve detailed verbal instructions, a larger maze to accommodate wheelchairs, and so on)?

SENSITIVITIES Games offer the perfect opportunity to explore issues such as diversity, respect, and communication. Consider any particularly touchy issues that might relate to the game before playing. Be prepared to set the game up, lead the activity, and debrief it in a safe way. Are group members:

- Comfortable with the physical interaction required by the game?

- Mature enough to talk and listen openly to one another without laughing, snickering, and belittling? If not, do you need to select a different activity, or enlist the support of additional caring adults who will help maintain a safe environment?

- Accepting of playing games in mixed-gender groups? Single-gender groups?

- Does the group have "touchy" issues related to the game?

GROUP SIZE Game success can depend on the number of participants. If your group is too large or small for a particular game, could you:

- Split into smaller groups or combine several groups and recruit additional game leaders?

- Adapt the game to fit the group size?

What Materials Do You Need?

PREPARATION Before game time, gather, as necessary, any of the following:

- Props (e.g., tennis balls, soft fabric balls, chart paper and markers, stopwatch, bandanas, string, masking tape, nametags)

- Paper and pens for note-taking

- Coaches, judges, supporters, demonstrators

- Any particular clothing (let players know if they need to dress a certain way—no heels or skirts, for instance)

When Are You Playing?

TIME PARAMETERS Suggested time ranges are provided for each game in this book. The time your group may require can depend on several factors, including who's in the group, how many people are playing, and how much time you have. Make sure to include enough time for playing the game, as well as for asking reflection questions. Ask yourself:

- How much time can we take to play a game?

- Is the game quick to learn, or does it take more explaining and practicing?

- Does the game require a lengthy debriefing session related to sensitive issues that arise?

ENERGY LEVEL Games in this book range from calm and quiet to loud and active. Think through your agenda and what you'll be doing. Do you need to:

- Boost energy in the middle of a meeting or class?

- Focus your group's attention?

- Fill the whole day?

Where Are You Playing?

INDOORS OR OUTDOORS You can play most of the games in this book indoors or outdoors, but keep in mind weather conditions that might affect plans. Be sure to locate available bathrooms. If it's hot outside, remember to bring water bottles. Consider the following:

- Is the area large enough for the group?

- Are tree roots, broken glass, or holes in the way?
  Are structural columns or furniture blocking the space?
  Are there exposed nails or other hazards to be avoided?

- Will your group's noise disturb others?
  Is the space quiet enough for participants to focus?

- Are the acoustics good?

TAKING RISKS

The games in this book are divided into three categories of physical and emotional risk: low, medium, and high. The need for group trust and comfort increases as the risk of the game increases, so carefully plan games sequentially. Be sensitive to the personalities of your group members and offer encouragement to shy, insecure, introverted, or new members, whose risk level may escalate more quickly than others. See the Game Index on page 219 for a summary of each game's risk level.

- **Low-risk games,** such as name games, scavenger hunts, and relays provide an opportunity for learning and growth without demanding significant personal risk.

- **Medium-risk games,** which often involve personal creativity, draw group members away from their comfort zone, but are nonthreatening to an individual's physical or emotional safety.

- **High-risk games,** like trust falls, require participants to trust one another significantly with their emotional and physical safety. These games mandate a solid foundation of group comfort, support, and time spent together.

Why Are You Playing?

GOALS Always identify the goals of your game and keep them in mind as you play. Use your goals as a framework for instructing, facilitating, and debriefing. Ask yourself:

- Do you want to play a game that sets the tone for a meeting or class or some other occasion?

- What do you want your group to achieve by the end of the game?

Establishing a solid foundation for group trust takes patience and understanding. Teams are no less than the individuals who make them up. Groups ebb and flow: They can be quiet and peaceful, or rush forward full tilt with great energy (whether from "storming," group dynamics, or innate high spirits). When individuals interact well and flow as a team, they can accomplish great things.

As you lead your group in playing the games in this book, embrace playfulness. No matter what stage of group development you're focusing on, trust the ebb and flow of individuals in your group. Play in and out of each stage as needed, and show participants you believe in their ability to achieve individual and team goals.

Don't forget to celebrate your group's accomplishments along the way. Celebration is a frequently neglected part of group building and is much needed. In fact, be sure to incorporate celebration games from Stage 6 throughout the team-building process. Celebrations can take place when new members join, when old members return, or when members successfully complete a task together—really, any individual or group success can be celebrated.

And people should also be celebrated for who they're becoming, for how they've grown together, and for what they've accomplished. Celebrations aren't just endings; they're also beginnings and relationship-maintenance, all at the same time. Just as the first stage in games-playing emphasizes the importance of starting the group off right, the final stage is a reminder of how important it is to contribute to the group's sense of positive identity.

Whether you work with groups of youth and adults in schools, neighborhoods, faith communities, or civic organizations, these games will energize your efforts and help you build the kind of relationships that help people thrive and have fun together. Are you ready to get started? Let the games begin! Play, celebrate, and have fun!

Stage 1

STARTING OFF RIGHT

Every group has a unique beginning. When you spend time from
the very start building a strong foundation, your group can avoid
typical pitfalls that get in the way of becoming a cohesive team.
Learning names is an important first step in establishing solid
relationships. Playing name games helps everyone learn names, get
better acquainted, and begin to feel comfortable as part of the group.
This first group development stage of game playing establishes the
importance of safety and respect in the group's work and play.

Name games can make it a breeze to remember names and
break down individual anxieties in the group. They create opportunities for group members to interact with people they wouldn't
naturally seek out, they help dissolve inhibitions and create a sense
of emotional safety and fun. When laughter enters into play, everyone
relaxes. The name games in this section range from paired activities
like "Share and Tell" (great for quiet, reserved groups or as a gentle
warm-up) to action-packed, laughter-guaranteed games like "Names
in Action." Name games are often quick, so you may choose to play
more than one in a single meeting to ensure that everyone really
learns names.

Tips for Leading Name Games

Keep these goals in mind when you lead name games:

- Learn and use players' names often to actively engage everyone.

- Get to know your group. (Keep paper and pen handy; jot down key words to identify players.)

- Make everyone feel welcome. Briefly talk with all players to engage them one-on-one.

- Establish ground rules from the start that will ensure the group's safety and respect for each other, and set a positive tone for each gathering.

- Play more than one name game if necessary, or play the same game on more than one occasion.

- Ask periodically if anyone can remember all the names in the group. Names begin to stick in everyone's memories as people go around the circle reciting them.

- Invite a group member who is especially good at remembering names to share memory tips at the end of the first name game or gathering.

THE FUN "ASSET"

The games in this book are geared toward having fun and laughing with others. When there's fun, positive relationships can develop readily. An essential asset for any group, having fun helps solidify relationships and build group identity.

NAME GAMES

Ask the following reflection questions with all the name games in this section to help groups process the importance of learning names and getting to know others well. Additional "Going Deeper" questions are provided after individual games that explore learning names even further.

- Why is it important to get to know others in a group?

- What is the most challenging part of meeting new people?

- In what kinds of situations do you find it most difficult to introduce yourself?

- How does learning and using people's names make you feel comfortable and welcome in a group?

- How is working together on a project or task easier when you know at least a few individuals' names?

SINGING NAMES

TIME 5–30 minutes

SAFETY NOTE Acknowledge the creative risk it takes to be bold. Allow a few moments for participants to think of what they want to do with their name. If no one wants to be first, then as the leader, go to it!

THE GAME Ask players to introduce themselves to the group by singing their name, using any spontaneous melody that comes to mind. Have the group sing back the name to the same tune to affirm the person and solidify the name for themselves.

ASSET CATEGORIES
Support, Empowerment, Constructive Use of Time, Social Competencies

NAMES IN ACTION

TIME 10–30 minutes

THE GAME Ask players to introduce themselves to the group, one by one, by pairing each syllable of their name with a fun motion as they say their name out loud. (For example, Crystal has two syllables in her name, so she puts her hands on her hips when she says *Crys* and bobs her head with *tal*.) The group responds to each person by repeating the name with the same action to affirm the person and learn the name for themselves. As each new person introduces herself or himself, ask the group to also repeat each previous person's name and action.

VARIATION *(for the brave, bold, and those who want to have fun!)*
After everyone has introduced themselves to the group, play a dance music compilation and call out names of group members at random. Everyone dances to the motions of each name as you call it out.

ASSET CATEGORIES
Support, Empowerment, Constructive Use of Time, Social Competencies

SLAP, CLAP, SNAP!

TIME 20–50 minutes

THE GAME Gather the group in a circle. Teach the group a steady rhythm to repeat the entire game. For example, slap thighs twice, clap hands twice, and snap fingers twice—once with the right hand and once with the left. Let the group practice: slap slap, clap clap, snap snap. Instruct participants to pause briefly between each movement to keep the beat steady and not too fast.

Once the group masters the rhythm and movements, appoint a starting person to say his name on the first snap and someone else's name on the second snap (or also point their snapping fingers at the person whose name they're calling). The person whose name is called must then say her name on the next snap and add someone else's name to the follow up snap, keeping the rhythm going.

Tell the group that the goal is to continue the pattern without changing, stopping, or missing a beat. If a player fumbles and says her name on the wrong beat or fails to call another name, she moves to another spot in the circle to help ensure that players are really learning names and not simply matching a name with a spot. Play can continue indefinitely.

ASSET CATEGORIES
Support, Empowerment, Constructive Use of Time, Social Competencies

TOSS-A-NAME

TIME 10–30 minutes

SUPPLIES
> Tennis or soft rubber ball (1 ball per group of 8–12)

THE GAME Divide players into small groups of 8–12 people, providing a ball for each group. Designate a leader for each group and instruct leaders to kick off the game by saying their names and passing the ball to either side. Continuing in order around the circle, each person is to say his or her name before passing the ball to the next player. Once the ball makes its way back to the leader, the leader may call anyone's name and gently toss the ball to that person. Players continue passing the ball to anyone, as long as they call a person's name before tossing the ball.

After several successful rounds, ask for volunteers (three or four) from each circle to change groups. Begin the ball toss again. After several minutes, tell everyone they can move at any time to any group. After the chaos of leaving and joining groups, have the groups form one large group and see who can name all the players in the circle.

ASSET CATEGORIES
Social Competencies, Constructive Use of Time, Support, Empowerment

IT'S YOUR BIRTHDAY

TIME 10–15 minutes

SUPPLIES
> CD, radio, or tape player

THE GAME Say to the group, "Pretend today is your birthday and everyone here is a guest at your party! To make sure everyone feels welcome, introduce as many people to each other as possible." To make the atmosphere festive, play music as people mingle. Allow 10 minutes for mingling and then ask for a show of hands to determine who introduced the most people. ("Who introduced 5? 6? 10?")

ASSET CATEGORIES Support, Social Competencies, Empowerment

NAME PULSE

TIME 5–15 minutes

SUPPLIES
> Stopwatch or watch with second hand

THE GAME Gather players in a circle. The goal is for every player to say his or her name as quickly as possible, one at a time, going in order around the circle. Choose someone to start the name pulse and the direction in which it will go. The first person says her name, the next person says his name, and so on around the circle. A player cannot say her name until the previous player finishes saying his. After a trial run, challenge the group to improve their time. Give them a few moments to figure out how they might be able to cut their time down. Let the group repeat the game several more times.

NOTE Players are shrewd. They may come up with ideas that seem "iffy," such as using abbreviations or the first letter or first syllable of their name. Let the group decide if they want to use shortcuts!

ASSET CATEGORIES Social Competencies, Support, Empowerment

SILENT SCRAMBLE

TIME 10–15 minutes

THE GAME Have players form a circle and, one by one, say their first names only once. Then ask players to put themselves in alphabetical order without communicating verbally!

GOING DEEPER
> What was necessary to put yourselves in order?
> How did you begin to know what to do?
> What specific role did you take in completing the task?

ASSET CATEGORIES Support, Social Competencies, Empowerment

BUMPITY, BUMP BUMP BUMP!

TIME 10–15 minutes

THE GAME Direct players to form a circle, share their first names with the group, and remember the names of players to their left and right. Designate a game leader to stand in the center of the circle, point to a player at random, and say "right" (or "left"). Within three seconds, that player must say the name of the person to the right (or left). If the leader points and says "bumpity, bump bump bump!" the player has to name people on *both* sides. If a player doesn't say the name or names quickly enough, he or she trades places with the leader in the center.

GOING DEEPER
> In what ways, if any, did the game cause stress or anxiety?
> Describe other situations when you've experienced similar feelings? How did you respond?
> What strategies did you use to succeed in this game?

ASSET CATEGORIES Social Competencies, Support, Empowerment

BEHIND EVERY NAME

TIME 20–40 minutes

SUPPLIES
> Small lightweight ball
> Chart paper or whiteboard
> Marker

THE GAME Have the group circle up (sitting or standing). Toss the ball around (or across) the circle. When players catch the ball, they should answer the following questions:

> What is your name?
> Are you named for a particular person or reason?
  If so, who or for what reason?
> Do you like or dislike your name?
  Explain why or tell what you'd like to be called.
> Where were you born?
> What is important to you about your heritage?
> What one thing would people be surprised to know about you?
> What are you proud of?

NOTE List questions on chart paper for everyone to keep in mind. Encourage players to contribute what they're comfortable sharing with others.

GOING DEEPER
> What did you discover about others in the group?
  About the various things you're proud of?
> Did you discover anything you have in common with others that you didn't realize before? Explain.
> How does your family heritage enrich your life?

ASSET CATEGORIES Social Competencies, Positive Identity

THE NAME GAME

TIME 20–30 minutes

THE GAME Draw players into a circle and ask them questions such as "What's your favorite ice cream flavor?" "What's your favorite way to relax?" or "What's your favorite thing about your home?" In turn, each player says his or her name and answers the given question. Guide the group's responses to players' answers. Emphasize respectful listening and positive affirmations without passing negative judgments.

GOING DEEPER

> Why do you feel differently about a group when they know your name and something about you?

> Why is it so powerful when other people remember our names?

> How does knowing a person's favorite thing help you to remember their name?

> Does knowing a person's name show that you honor and respect them? How?

ASSET CATEGORIES
Commitment to Learning, Support, Social Competencies, Empowerment

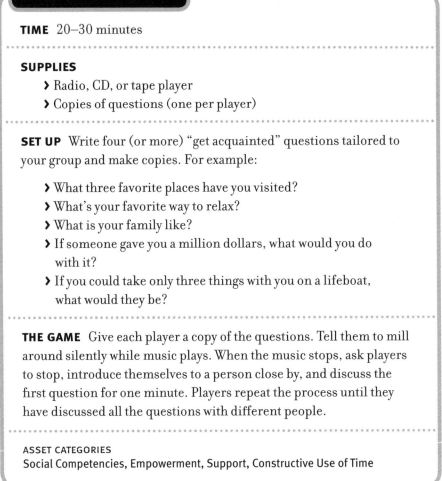

MILLING TO MUSIC

TIME 20–30 minutes

SUPPLIES
> Radio, CD, or tape player
> Copies of questions (one per player)

SET UP Write four (or more) "get acquainted" questions tailored to your group and make copies. For example:

> What three favorite places have you visited?
> What's your favorite way to relax?
> What is your family like?
> If someone gave you a million dollars, what would you do with it?
> If you could take only three things with you on a lifeboat, what would they be?

THE GAME Give each player a copy of the questions. Tell them to mill around silently while music plays. When the music stops, ask players to stop, introduce themselves to a person close by, and discuss the first question for one minute. Players repeat the process until they have discussed all the questions with different people.

ASSET CATEGORIES
Social Competencies, Empowerment, Support, Constructive Use of Time

SHARE AND TELL

TIME 20–30 minutes

SUPPLIES
> Masking tape
> Scrap paper
> Pen or pencil for each participant

SET UP Tape a small piece of paper on each person's back.

THE GAME Have players sit in two concentric circles with those in the inner circle facing those in the outer circle and have them pair up. Give each person one minute to tell his or her partner as much about himself or herself as possible. Encourage participants to talk about something they're proud of, what they love to do or learn about, or an obstacle they've overcome. Instruct the listener to write one positive word describing the speaker (or something wonderful they've noticed about the speaker) on the paper taped to the speaker's back.

Direct players to switch roles and then ask those in the outer circle to shift two places to the left so everyone has a new partner. Rotate until everyone has partnered with 4–6 different people. Have the last set of partners remove their papers and read to themselves.

GOING DEEPER
> How does it feel to talk about yourself?
> How often do you listen closely to others and really hear what they're saying?
> How did it feel to read the positive words others wrote on your back?
> What did you learn about perceptions other people have of you?
> How can you be more intentional about building friendships with people in the future?

ASSET CATEGORIES
Positive Values, Positive Identity, Social Competencies, Empowerment, Support

THAT'S ME!

TIME 5–10 minutes

SUPPLIES
> Index cards (one per player)
> Pen or pencil (one per player)
> Chart paper or white board

NOTE This activity works well to break up a long retreat, after several hours of activities, or over time at the beginning of meetings to spotlight individual participants. Save it to use after breaks or for a change of pace.

SET UP Write the following questions and sample responses on chart paper, and make enough copies for each player.

> What do you have in common with most people in the group? (*Sample answer: I walk on two legs.*)
> What do you have in common with some people in the group? (*Sample answer: I was born in a big city.*)
> What is something you have in common with a few people in the group? (*Sample answer: I wear contact lenses.*)
> What is something unique to you? (*Sample answer: I have a fishing-hook scar on my left ankle.*)

THE GAME Give each player an index card and pencil and ask them to answer the questions. Collect cards and ask the group to stand. Select one card. Read the first question, and ask who shares the answer given on the card you chose. Players should sit down (and remain seated) if the answer doesn't apply to them. Continue reading aloud answers on the card to the second and third questions. As each response is read, more and more players are likely to sit down. The game usually narrows by the fourth question to the one person whose trait is unique in the group. Announce the name of the person who remains standing. Invite everyone to stand again and repeat as time allows.

GOING DEEPER
> In what ways did this activity get you thinking about what you have in common with others?

> How often do you take time to look for similarities between yourself and your teammates?
> Why is it important to appreciate your uniqueness as well?
> How can you be intentional about building friendships?

ASSET CATEGORIES Positive Identity, Support

TEAM BANNERS

TIME 20–30 minutes

SUPPLIES
> Poster board or butcher paper
> Markers

NOTE You can adapt this game for use as a closing activity by having players create a banner that depicts their group "bests" (see "Stage 6" on page 195).

THE GAME Direct participants to make a group banner that highlights members' characteristics: hobbies, hometowns, summer plans, likes, and dislikes. Encourage them to draw images, too. Other ideas to list or draw include: favorite gift, meal, surprise, vacation, or family story. Suggest banner topics based on information you'd like group members to learn about one another. Post the completed banner where everyone can see it.

VARIATION Divide the group into smaller teams of four. Ask each group to create a banner on poster board, highlighting with words and images information about the following topics:

> Names
> Something all four players have in common
> A group name that collectively describes them (or their view of life)
> Something unique about each individual

Have each group share their banner and tell what they learned about each other. This activity helps groups recognize the positive attributes of their wider community.

GOING DEEPER

> What did you learn about one another's backgrounds, cultures, and differences?
> What new commonalities did you discover about your teammates?
> How did this activity help you begin to build support for each other and boost your own self-image?

ASSET CATEGORIES Support, Social Competencies, Positive Identity

STICKY IDS

TIME 20–25 minutes

SUPPLIES

> Self-sticking note paper and pens

THE GAME Give each participant a sheet of paper and a pen. Ask them to draw two lines (making a "+") to divide their paper into four squares. Have them fill in each section with answers to the following prompts:

List something you liked doing when you were younger that you still enjoy.	List one of your favorite things to do outside.
List a career you might like to explore.	List a place you'd love to visit one day.

Ask participants to pair up with someone they don't know well and take two minutes to share what they wrote. Have participants repeat the process with 5–6 more partners. Ask the group to form a circle and share some of the things they learned about each other.

GOING DEEPER

> While talking with others in the group, what other fun activities did you think of that you especially enjoy?
> What other careers did you hear about that interested you?
> Name something memorable that you learned about a teammate.

ASSET CATEGORIES Support, Commitment to Learning, Empowerment, Social Competencies, Constructive Use of Time

CROSSWORD CONNECTIONS

TIME 15–20 minutes

SUPPLIES

> Paper and pens (graph paper with large squares works well)

THE GAME Give each person a pen and paper on which they write their name across the center of the page. Ask everyone to mingle for 5–10 minutes, searching for common connections with others in the group (e.g., both have the same hobby, both speak more than one language). Players connect their name, crossword style, to the names of others with whom they share common interests and write the shared interest nearby in parentheses. If player's names can't connect to the letters of another person's name, tell them to search for other connections and return when letter combinations allow them to connect. See how many connections everyone can find.

GOING DEEPER

> How does finding commonalities affect your comfort level in a group?
> Do you take time to find commonalities with others in everyday life? Why or why not?
> Does finding commonalities make it easier to start conversations? Build relationships?

ASSET CATEGORIES
Social Competencies, Empowerment, Boundaries and Expectations, Support

THE MATCHING GAME

TIME 20–40 minutes

SUPPLIES
> Paper and pens

SET UP Prepare a list of questions pertinent to all players, such as the following:

> What is your partner's favorite book?
> What would your partner say is his or her best trait: smile, personality, or ability to listen?
> What would your partner say is the best part about getting older?
> What movie has the most important message your partner has ever seen?
> What issue means a lot to your partner?
> What does your partner think people spend too much time worrying about?
> Would your partner choose pizza or hamburgers?
> What color are your partner's eyes?
> What type of music does your partner like best?
> How many siblings does your partner have?
> What subject in school is your partner's best?
> Which superhero would your partner say he or she is most like: Batman, Spiderman, Superman, or Wonder Woman?

Provide enough questions to cover two rounds of play, with four or five questions for each round. If the group is large, ask some group members to play the role of spectators, designate some to keep score for each team, and have a couple keep watch at the door to tell the other group when to come back into the room.

THE GAME Tell players they're going to find out just how well they know each other. Teams that answer the most questions correctly win. Divide the group into pairs. Ask each pair to determine who in the pair will stay and who will leave the room. Consider asking another leader to wait with the players who temporarily leave while the other players get ready.

Ask remaining players to answer questions one at a time the way they think their partner would respond. Have each person answer aloud and write their answer on the paper. When everyone has answered, call their partners back to the room. Ask the returning players to sit in front of their partners with their backs to them to avoid facial communication. Ask returning players to answer aloud each question asked of their partners. Partners reveal their written responses. Award one point to pairs for each matching answer. Switch roles and go through a second round with a new set of questions. The team with the most matches wins the "Friendship Award."

GOING DEEPER

> What did you like best about this activity?
> Were there any surprises? What were they?
> How well did most pairs know each other?
> Once you get to know someone pretty well, in what ways do you actively continue to learn more about each other?
> How can you apply the lessons of this game to your family?
> What questions could you ask to get to know your family better?

ASSET CATEGORIES
Social Competencies, Constructive Use of Time, Support, Empowerment

TAKE A HIKE

TIME 10–20 minutes

SUPPLIES
> Masking tape

SET UP Place tape marks on the floor in a circle (one less mark than the number of people in the group).

SAFETY NOTE Remind participants not to push others when rushing to find a new spot.

THE GAME Have participants (except for one volunteer in the middle of the circle) stand on a piece of tape. Ask the volunteer to state something outrageous or unique about her- or himself (or the group), such as "I've gone caving." Players who identify with the statement "take a hike" and scramble (along with the volunteer) to find another spot around the circle.

When everyone has moved, the odd person out takes the volunteer's place in the middle and a new round begins. Keep going until everyone has shared something fun and unique about themselves.

GOING DEEPER
> What surprising true things did you discover about each other?
> How can you apply what you learned in this game to foster friendships?
> How can your group create an atmosphere that makes it easy to share thoughts, talents, and experiences with each other?

ASSET CATEGORIES
Social Competencies, Empowerment, Support, Positive Identity

IN THE SPOTLIGHT

TIME 10–40 minutes

SUPPLIES
> Box or bag
> Pens and small note paper

THE GAME Have each participant write down one question he or she would like to ask anyone in the group (and that would be willingly answered). Questions should be G-rated and can cover a variety of appropriate topics, such as "What do you do for fun?" "What do you like or dislike about school?" or "If you could change one thing about your community, what would it be and why?" Encourage creativity and thoughtfulness. Put all questions in the box. Have players take turns drawing a question and answering it. Once a player answers a question, allow other players time to ask follow-up questions.

GOING DEEPER
> Did you discover you had more in common with anyone than you realized?
> How does it feel to be "in the spotlight"?
> What did you learn from this game about taking time to listen to others?

ASSET CATEGORIES Social Competencies, Support, Positive Values

FOUR ON A COUCH

TIME 10–20 minutes

SUPPLIES
> Paper and pens
> Box or bag
> Chairs arranged in a circle (one chair more than the number of players; four of the chairs aligned in a straight "couch")

THE GAME Divide the group into two teams (splitting into teams of boys and girls works well if numbers are even) and ask players to sit. Ask each person to write his or her first name on a slip of paper and fold it in half. Collect slips in the box, mix them up, and have each person draw their "new" name. The object is to seat four members of the same team on the "couch," using their new names.

The player to the left of the empty chair goes first and calls the name of a player other than the one he or she has drawn. Whoever has drawn that name moves to the empty chair. The person to the left of the new empty chair calls out a second name. Encourage players to keep in mind the "new" names of players on each team so that they can eventually place their teammates on the "couch." Play continues until one of the teams seats four of its members in a row on the couch.

GOING DEEPER
> What was hard about the game?
> What strategies did you use to get all four of your team members on the couch?
> How did you remember the new identities of your team?

ASSET CATEGORIES Social Competencies, Support, Commitment to Learning

PEEK-A-WHO?

TIME 15–45 minutes

SUPPLIES
> Thick blanket or shower curtain

THE GAME Designate two leaders to hold the blanket up like a curtain and split remaining players into two groups. Place one group on each side of the blanket. Each group quietly chooses one person to kneel close to the blanket. When the leaders drop the blanket to the floor, the first person in the kneeling pair to call out the name of the other person scores a team point. The second person joins the winning team. Play continues until one team has captured the other team. If team members know each other well, the kneeling pair can sit with their backs to the blanket. When the leaders drop the blanket to the floor, the pair must rely on verbal clues from their group members to guess each other's identity. All clues must be framed as positive attributes, respecting each person's diversity, abilities, and self-worth.

GOING DEEPER
> How much time did it take to capture the other team?
> If you lost a round, what strategies did you use next time to name someone?
> How does it feel to hear positive comments made about you?
> In what ways can you work to build others' self-esteem?

ASSET CATEGORIES Social Competencies, Empowerment, Positive Identity

LICENSE PLATES

TIME 15–20 minutes

SUPPLIES
> Colored paper
> Markers

THE GAME Give participants colored paper and markers. Ask them to create a personalized license plate or bumper sticker that reflects their personality and interests. Ask players to share their creations. Encourage them to play with words, unique spelling, and catchy icons.

GOING DEEPER

> In what ways was it difficult or easy to celebrate your uniqueness?
> Why is it important to let your friends, family, and others know the "real you"?

ASSET CATEGORIES Positive Identity, Constructive Use of Time, Support

MYSTERY PARTNERS

TIME 30 minutes

SUPPLIES
> Note cards and pens or pencils

THE GAME Give each player a note card and pen. Instruct them to list three of their favorite hobbies or things to do and not share what they've written. Ask them also to draw a picture (stick figures are fine) or identify themselves with a symbol that represents their interests. Collect and shuffle the cards. Distribute a card to each person and give each player an opportunity to guess the name of his or her "mystery partner." If a player guesses correctly, allow their mystery partner to comment on what he or she wrote. If a guess is incorrect, ask the mystery person to reveal his or her identity. Continue until all players identify or learn their mystery partner's identity.

GOING DEEPER

> What clued you in on your mystery partner's identity?
> Why is it important to have a good self-image?
> How can you help yourself and others build a positive identity?

ASSET CATEGORIES Support, Constructive Use of Time, Positive Values, Social Competencies, Positive Identity, Empowerment

Stage 2

BUILDING RELATIONSHIPS

Building and strengthening relationships is a part of all stages of group formation, but this is where it really takes off. As groups change in size or add new members, frequently replaying the relationship-building games in this section lets friendships develop and group connections solidify.

Relationship-building games help a group bond, reinforce the importance of safety, and establish group identity. These games typically require minimal critical thinking skills and create group energy by getting the blood flowing, hearts pumping, and worries easing away. Goals for relationship-building games include helping players get to know each other better and feel more comfortable as part of a particular group.

Choose games for your group based on your goals:

- Do players need to burn off energy with a relay?

- Do you need to create group energy?

- Do players need to get to know each other better by doing a scavenger hunt?

Be sure to intersperse name games with games in this stage so that you reinforce the value of *really* getting to know each other.

Tips for Leading Relationship-Building Games

As you play games at this early stage of group development and identity, keep these tips in mind:

- Set firm expectations regarding behavior to ensure safe, fun play and prevent participants from getting carried away from play toward chaos.

- Make it clear to participants when they are to listen to you giving directions and stating rules, and when they can begin to play.

- Ask players to respect one another's ideas and contributions, avoid put-downs, and encourage their teammates.

- To gradually gain a group's trust and get all participants pumped up, it's often useful to start with a quieter game, such as "Who's the Leader?" and build from there.

- If players test your limits, restate expectations and return to quieter games before trying high energy games.

ZIP BONG

TIME 20 minutes

THE GAME Have players sit in a circle, and choose one person to start the game. Tell players to face the player on their left and say "zip" one at a time, going around the circle clockwise as fast as possible. As they say "zip," they have to keep their teeth completely covered with their lips (no smiling)! Warn the group that if players accidentally show any teeth, they'll be out.

Once players understand the "zip," add a new movement. Players can reverse the direction of play by turning to the player on their right and saying "bong." The player receiving the "bong" can either continue in the new direction (saying "zip") or can reverse the direction again (by saying "bong"). Players who show their teeth, look in the wrong direction, or go too slowly, must step out of the circle and become judges. The competitive and speedy play continues until the circle shrinks to two players, the winners.

GOING DEEPER

> How difficult or easy was it for you to stay focused and not laugh?

> Why is it healthy for a group to laugh together?

> How does laughing with other people help build relationships?

ASSET CATEGORIES Positive Values, Social Competencies, Positive Identity

ZOOM

TIME 20 minutes

THE GAME Direct players to sit in a circle, and choose one person to lead. Tell players they are to look at their neighbor and say "zoom!" one at a time, going left around the circle (clockwise) as fast as possible.

Players can reverse the direction of play by turning to the player on their right and saying "wacka zoom!" The player on the right continues the game, passing the "zoom" in the new direction.

Players can also pass the "zoom" to a player on the opposite side of the circle by saying "super zoom" as they point to that person. Practice a few rounds and then begin the game. If a person makes a mistake by using the wrong command or looks at the wrong player when passing the "zoom," that player must step out of the circle. Play continues until there are two remaining players, the winners.

GOING DEEPER
> What helps you respond quickly to challenges?
> What helps you make quick decisions under pressure?
> In what ways are you a creature of habit?
> In what kinds of situations do you feel comfortable trying new things?

ASSET CATEGORIES
Social Competencies, Commitment to Learning, Constructive Use of Time

WHO'S THE LEADER?

TIME 5-15 minutes

THE GAME Choose one person to be "it" and leave the room. Choose a second person to lead remaining players sitting in a circle. The leader starts a simple motion that everyone else follows together, such as slapping hands against the knees, and then changes the motions periodically. Direct players (before "it" returns) to avoid staring at the leader and revealing his or her identity. "It" comes back to the circle and has three guesses to try to name the leader. If "it" guesses correctly, the leader becomes the new "it." If "it" doesn't guess correctly, he or she remains "it" for another round.

GOING DEEPER
> How challenging was it to be the leader?
> How challenging was it to be a part of the group and not give the leader away?
> How challenging was it to be "it"?
> How important is cooperation in the group?

ASSET CATEGORIES Social Competencies, Support

YOU'RE A STAR!

TIME 10–30 minutes

SUPPLIES
> Index cards (one per player)
> Masking tape

SET UP Write the name of a famous person on each index card—real or fictional, living or from the past. Choose names the group will know (movie, cartoon, and comic book heroes work well, along with famous musicians and figures from history).

THE GAME Tape a card to each player's back without showing the player the name written on it. Tell players to mingle, asking one another "yes/no" questions until everyone figures out their secret identity. If you want to make the game competitive, say that the first person to correctly guess his or her new name wins the game. Or have players keep track of how many questions they must ask to guess their new name. The winner is the player who guesses correctly and asks the least number of questions.

GOING DEEPER
> What did you learn about asking questions to uncover hidden information?
> In what ways was it difficult for you to talk to people you didn't know well?
> What lessons can you apply from this game to meeting new people?
> How might you continue getting to know others in our group?

ASSET CATEGORIES Social Competencies, Constructive Use of Time

LEADERSHIP LINE-UP

TIME 5–20 minutes

THE GAME Give players one minute to line up in their birthday order (from January 1 to December 31) without talking or mouthing words. Have players raise their hands when everyone thinks they're standing in the correct order. Starting at one end, confirm everyone's birthdays to see if the group did put themselves correctly in order.

VARIATION Give the group new leadership tasks. These work well when you want to split into smaller groups. Line up alphabetically by first name, number of siblings, hair color, number of pets, number of years in your group—use your imagination! After everyone has lined up, you can number them off for the next group task.

GOING DEEPER
> What leadership decisions have to be made in order to complete any task?
> What decisions did your group make to complete the line-up?
> How well did your group work together? What would you do differently?

ASSET CATEGORIES   Empowerment, Social Competencies, Positive Identity

HOG CALL

TIME 20 minutes

SUPPLIES
> Index cards (at least one per player)

NOTE This game works especially well in a large group (more than 20), as it presents appropriate challenge when players try to find their partner.

SET UP The group can be enlisted to create word pairs for the game, if you want to avoid preparation beforehand. Create sets of paired or compound word cards (at least one card per player), writing one part of the word pair on one card (for example, "peanut") and the other part on another card ("butter"). A sample list might include ice cream, rock star, rug rat, bookworm, hip hop, and so on. Players can get silly and make up fun pairs or compounds. Saying them aloud beforehand helps players make sense of the word pairs as they play.

THE GAME Shuffle the cards and give everyone one card. When you give the cue, ask participants to hunt for their compound word partners. When players believe they've found their partner, ask them to stand next to their partner and form a large circle. The group may need to problem solve and shuffle partners around, because some words will present multiple compound possibilities for their partners.

GOING DEEPER
> What decision-making strategies did you use to succeed in this game?
> If your word made more than one compound word, how did you sort through the possibilities to find your word partner?
> How might this game apply to real life?

ASSET CATEGORIES
Constructive Use of Time, Social Competencies, Positive Identity

YOU BELONG!

TIME 15–20 minutes

THE GAME Ask players to form groups as quickly as possible as you call out the different criteria:

> › Form a group of two players; now four; now six.
> › Form a group of six people wearing athletic shoes
>   (or a particular shoe color).
> › Form a group of people in which at least one person wears
>   red socks (or no socks).
> › Form a group of people wearing red shirts, white shirts,
>   and blue shirts (or another color pattern at your discretion).
> › Find a person who shares your birthday month, and sing "Happy
>   birthday to us!"
> › Form a group of three, each with the same eye color
>   (for variety, make it each with a different eye color).
> › Form groups of morning people and late night owls.

Do this several times. Keep the pace fast!

GOING DEEPER

> › What other groupings would be interesting to explore?
> › What new information, if any, did you learn about others
>   in the group?
> › Why is it important to recognize the wide range of subgroups
>   that exist within our group? Any group?

ASSET CATEGORIES Social Competencies, Positive Identity

IMPULSE

TIME 15 minutes

THE GAME Ask players to stand in a circle and hold hands loosely. Choose a leader to send a gentle hand squeeze ("impulse") travel-ing clockwise around the circle. Tell the group they should pass the impulse as fast as they can without skipping players and commenting on their progress. Their goal is to complete the circuit and return the impulse to the leader in as short a time as possible. For added challenge, ask players to play with their eyes closed. After the impulse has traveled successfully around the group, try sending two simultaneously in opposite directions, returning to the leader on both sides.

VARIATION Have players sit cross-legged, knee-to-knee, in a circle with their hands resting on their neighbors' knees. Choose a leader to start a gentle clockwise knee tap. Challenge the group to send the knee tap around the circle as quickly as possible with no mistakes and without talking, ending the round with the leader. Try again with a new leader. For extra challenge, try two knee taps moving in opposite directions and have players close their eyes.

GOING DEEPER

> What, if anything, was frustrating about this game?
> What does this game teach about teamwork?
> Why is it important to stay focused to complete a task?
> What happened when the pulse went in two directions at once? How did you handle the challenge?

ASSET CATEGORIES
Support, Empowerment, Positive Values, Social Competencies

MINI-SCAVENGER HUNT

TIME 10–15 minutes

THE GAME Think of items that players are likely to have on hand (e.g., sticks of gum, sunglasses, keys, paperbacks, and backpack carabiners). Also think of group strengths (e.g. athletes and artists), and use the items and strengths as the basis for a fun, spontaneous scavenger hunt.

Ask players to form groups of 4–6. Players should have their backpacks, purses, wallets, jackets, and gym bags on hand. Call out the list to each group and give the signal to start the mini-scavenger hunt. The round ends when one group collects all items on the list. After five rounds, applaud the group that found the most items.

GOING DEEPER

> What did you learn from this game?
> How are we resources to each other?
> Why is it important to work together and lean on each other?
> Do you ask others for help when you need it?
  Do you willingly help others? Why or why not?
> If you had played this game by yourself, how do you think it would have been easier? More difficult?

ASSET CATEGORIES Support, Empowerment, Social Competencies

THE SMILING GAME

TIME 10 minutes

SUPPLIES
> Watch with second hand

SAFETY NOTE Remind players that appropriate behavior is expected of them. If the group is not comfortable with physical contact or is not well-acquainted, set boundaries regarding what kinds of touching is allowed in order to elicit smiles.

THE GAME Ask players to sit in a circle and choose one person to be "it." "It" is to walk around the circle and try to get players to smile or laugh within 10 seconds by making funny faces or goofy sounds or saying something humorous—whatever it takes! The player being encouraged to smile must try to keep a straight face and respond, "I'm not falling for it!" If the other player does laugh or smile, that person becomes the new "it." If "it" fails, he or she moves on to a new victim!

VARIATION Divide players into two lines facing each other. The two teams form the "laughing gauntlet." One player from each team stands at opposite ends of the gauntlet facing each other. They bow to each other, calling "hagoo" ("come here" in the language of the Alaskan Flingit Indians, inventors of the game). The two players walk toward each other, maintain eye contact, and then pass, continuing on to the opposite end of the laughing gauntlet. They must do this without laughing or giggling and keep a straight face the entire time.

Meanwhile, the two opposing teams heckle and try their best to make the challenger from the opposite team laugh. (No touching allowed!) Challengers who successfully walk the gauntlet without smiling or laughing may rejoin their team. Unsuccessful challengers must join the opposing team. The game ends when there is only one team, or when players can take no more. This game allows everyone to try his or her best jokes, silliest laughs, and goofiest faces in an appropriate setting. It's an excellent exercise in self-control.

GOING DEEPER

> How important is it to bring joy into other people's lives by encouraging them to laugh?

> What kind actions can you take to help others laugh and enjoy daily life?

> When you feel stressed or at odds with someone, what can you do to lighten things up?

> How do you practice the art of using humor at appropriate times and at other times remaining quiet when focus is needed?

ASSET CATEGORIES
Positive Values, Constructive Use of Time, Social Competencies, Empowerment

COLORFUL CONVERSATIONS

TIME 10–20 minutes

SUPPLIES
> Bag of small colored candies
> Copies of "Colorful Conversation Codes" chart (one per group)

THE GAME Pass a bag of colored candy to players gathered in a circle. Ask players to take a small handful of candies in as many different colors as possible. Be sure to tell players not to eat the candy until they hear the instructions. Divide the group into smaller groups of 3–5 players and pass out color code charts to each group. Ask each player to select one candy and compare its color to the conversation topics on the chart. Group members take turns responding to the topics and can eat their candy after each turn. Give players the opportunity to share at least three times with the group. Players not only learn about each other, but also think more about what is important to them.

GOING DEEPER
> What surprising or interesting things did you learn about each other?
> Why is it important to think about your opinions and tell others about them?
> How often do you share your opinions with others?
> How can you strike a balance between sharing too little and too much about yourself?

ASSET CATEGORIES Support, Boundaries and Expectations, Positive Identity, Social Competencies, Positive Values, Commitment to Learning

Colorful Conversation Codes

BLUE
Share a family fact, or complete the sentence:
"When I get home, I'm going to . . . ."

RED
Describe a favorite way to spend your time,
or complete the sentence:
"One challenge I overcame this week was . . . ."

ORANGE
Tell about something you're proud of, or complete the sentence:
"The most important thing I've learned this week is . . . ."

YELLOW
Describe someone you respect, or complete the sentence:
"I thought it was really great today when . . . ."

GREEN
Share a goal you have for your future, or complete the sentence:
"The best thing about my school (or job) is . . . ."

BROWN
Describe your favorite movie, or complete the sentence:
"The most meaningful part of this week has been . . . ."

Note: Change colors, if needed, to match candy.

ANIMAL CORNERS

TIME 10–20 minutes

SUPPLIES
> › Four sheets of paper
> › Masking tape
> › Marker

THE GAME Label each sheet of paper with one of these titles: "Lion," "Deer," "Fox," and "Dove" (you could also use "Mountain," "River," "Ocean," "Meadow," or "Piano," "Guitar," "Drum," and "Flute"). Tape one sign in each corner of the room. Ask players to stand under the sign they are most like when part of the group.

GOING DEEPER
> › Why did you choose this sign?
> › What choice would you make (and why) if you were with friends? Family? By yourself?
> › How difficult was it for you to choose?
> › How is taking a stand important for each of us?

ASSET CATEGORIES Social Competencies, Positive Identity

PERSONALITY SKETCHES

TIME 20 minutes

SUPPLIES
> › Flip chart paper and marker
> › Paper and pencils (one per player)

NOTE This game is strictly for fun and will generate lots of laughs! You can also use it to raise awareness of our tendency to jump to the wrong conclusion about people based on superficial information.

THE GAME Ask for a volunteer to sketch a pig on flip chart paper. Instruct participants to draw their own pig on paper but not look at their neighbors' sketches. Explain to players that their sketches represent one process—not at all accurate in this case!—of personality testing. Emphasize that this game just gives you an idea of the way a person *might* perceive images and is simply one way that people study and learn about how others think. Consider the following interpretations of sketches—but don't take them seriously!

If you drew the pig:

> Toward the top of your paper, you are a positive, optimistic person.
> Toward the middle of the page, you are a realist.
> Toward the bottom of the page, you are sometimes pessimistic.
> Facing left, you like tradition, are friendly, and remember dates and birthdays.
> Facing forward, you are direct and enjoy confronting issues head on.
> Facing right, you are innovative and active, but sometimes prefer being alone.
> With many details, you are analytical and cautious.
> With few details, you are emotional, care little for specifics, and take risks.
> With four legs showing, you are secure, stubborn, and stick to your ideals.
> With less than four legs showing, you are uncertain or in a period of change.
> With large ears, you are a good listener.
> With a long tail, you are happy with your friendships (with older players, you could change "friendships" to "love life" for a big laugh).

GOING DEEPER

> While this activity was just for fun, how might sketching, doodling, drawing, and painting reveal something about who you really are?
> In what ways can all the arts (including writing, playing music, dancing, singing) let you express important feelings?

ASSET CATEGORIES   Social Competencies, Constructive Use of Time

CONVERSATION STARTERS

BAG OF QUESTIONS

TIME 10–30 minutes

SUPPLIES
> Resealable bag
> Paper slips

SET UP Write questions to start conversations on slips of paper, and place them in a bag. For ideas, see "It's All in the Questions" on page 216.

NOTE This activity works well for a single session, but also can be used as a kick off for multiple gatherings of the group. It allows players to explore multiple issues and clarify their values, beliefs, and opinions.

THE GAME Ask players to draw a paper slip from the bag. The person who draws the question can answer first and then invite others to share their thoughts and get a conversation going.

GOING DEEPER
> How does it feel to be put on the spot?
> What strategies can you use to defuse the discomfort?
> Did you find points in common with members of your group?
> How does that change the way you feel about the group?
> What are respectful ways to disagree with people who offer opinions you don't share?

ASSET CATEGORIES
Positive Values, Positive Identity, Constructive Use of Time, Support

PAN GAME

TIME 10–20 minutes

SUPPLIES
> Noisemaker (e.g., stainless pan and spoon or whistle)
> Conversation-starter questions (for ideas, see "It's All in the Questions" on page 216)

THE GAME Ask participants to mingle and form as quickly as possible into groups equal in size to the number of times you hit the pan or blow the whistle. (Traditionally, anybody who doesn't make it into a group is out, but depending on the total number of participants, allow them to join a group.) Give each group a question to discuss. Repeat the process a few more rounds, changing how many times you hit the pan to form new groups. For the last round, hit the pan as many times as the number of players in the group. Pose one question for everyone to discuss.

GOING DEEPER
> What did you like about this activity? Dislike?
> What happens when one person dominates the conversation? Or when people don't respond to what you say?
> How can you be supportive of others when they share something important about themselves?

ASSET CATEGORIES Social Competencies, Positive Identity

FAMILY CHATTER

TIME 10–30 minutes

SUPPLIES
> Resealable bag
> Paper slips

SET UP Write conversation-starter questions on paper slips and place in a resealable bag (for ideas, see "It's All in the Questions" on page 216).

NOTE This is a great activity to kick off an intergenerational gathering, a PTA meeting, family night, and faith community gatherings. It encourages families and other groups to slow down, talk, and share with each other. Families can add questions to the pile and take copies of the questions home for use on family dinner nights.

THE GAME Have participants join their family or one other family to form a group and draw a question to discuss. Trade off having youth and adults choose the question.

GOING DEEPER

> In what ways do youth and adults think alike? Differently?
> How does this activity allow families to learn to communicate about beliefs and opinions, and clarify important values?
> What new things did you learn about your family (or others in your group)?

ASSET CATEGORIES
Support, Positive Identity, Constructive Use of Time, Commitment to Learning

TICKET TALK

TIME 20–30 minutes

SUPPLIES

> Roll of movie tickets
> Bag of small candy treats

THE GAME Give participants at least three tickets from the roll (they can take up to 10). Then ask each person to tell the group something about himself or herself for each ticket they took. If you have an especially large group, you might limit the sharing to 5–6 tickets. Let players redeem their tickets for candy prizes.

GOING DEEPER

> Did you surprise yourself by sharing something you hadn't talked about before?
> What did you enjoy learning about others in your group?

ASSET CATEGORIES   Support, Positive Identity, Social Competencies

TWO TRUTHS AND A LIE

TIME 15–30 minutes

SUPPLIES
> Paper and pencils

THE GAME Divide players into groups of three or four. Give them 10 minutes to write on a sheet of paper two statements that are true for all of them and one that is a lie for all of them. Ask each group to read their three statements without giving away which are true or false. Groups can reread their statements if needed. Then have remaining participants vote on which statement they believe is the lie. Groups that correctly identify the lie score a point. Continue until all teams have taken their turn. Play two more rounds. The group scoring the most points wins.

GOING DEEPER
> What helped you determine which statements were true and which were false?
> How difficult was it to come up with a realistic lie?
> How important is honesty in real life?
> Why is it sometimes difficult to be honest and tell the truth?

ASSET CATEGORIES Positive Values, Social Competencies

COMMON GROUND

TIME 10–30 minutes

SUPPLIES
> Paper and pens

THE GAME Split the group into four smaller groups and have them stand in four different corners or areas. Ask each group to list as many things as possible that members of the group have in common. Encourage them to think creatively. Give 10 minutes for each group of 12 people or more; give 4–5 minutes if groups have fewer than 12. When time is up, point to a group to quickly name one thing all members have in common. Continue rapidly around the room, giving each group three seconds to name another common trait. A group is out if they take longer than three seconds, repeat something another group has already said, or run out of things to say. Ask each group to count the number of items they have in common.

GOING DEEPER
> What was your group's strategy to determine the longest list?
> Did you find you had more in common than you thought you might? Why or why not?
> How do we often stereotype people, before trying to find common ground?
> In what ways can you learn about what people are really like?

ASSET CATEGORIES
Empowerment, Positive Values, Social Competencies, Positive Identity

TINY TEACH

TIME 20–30 minutes

SUPPLIES
> Chart paper
> Marker

NOTE Young people sometimes think they may not have any skills to teach, so the thought of teaching someone else can be intimidating. To keep this game low-risk, give participants simple lesson examples, such as teaching others how to shoot a free throw, perform a snowboard trick, fold a paper airplane, or bake cookies, or telling others about a subject they know well, such as collecting figurines or designing a Web site.

This activity is great for youth-adult partnerships because it emphasizes both youth and adults have something to offer and teach each other. Try pairing youth and adults together. Have the young person teach the adult first. Ask adults to share their new knowledge with the group, and then reverse the process.

THE GAME Divide the group into pairs. Set up the activity by noting that all are resources and have something to share with others. Give pairs at least 5 minutes to teach or tell each other about a subject they know well. Let players know you'll be asking for volunteers to share with the group. Allow additional time if players need it. Let as many groups volunteer to demonstrate or describe their new knowledge as time allows. Encourage shy participants and tell all players to be proud of what they know. Write on chart paper topics that are shared, and talk about what players have learned. Note the variety of things that were learned about the group and how everyone had something to share.

GOING DEEPER
> What surprised you about this activity?
> What did you learn about your own abilities?
> Why do you need to keep "digging deeper" to get to know and appreciate other players?

ASSET CATEGORIES Empowerment, Commitment to Learning, Social Competencies, Constructive Use of Time

DIVERSEGORIES

TIME 30–40 minutes

SUPPLIES
> Copies of "Diversegories Game Card"
> (one per group of 4–6)
> Pencils

SET UP Make copies of the "Diversegories Game Card" or use it to create your own game card with diversity categories that make sense for your group.

THE GAME Have participants form groups of 4–6 players. Give each group 20 minutes to fill in information in each of the categories on their game card. Explore the diversity within groups, using the reflection questions.

GOING DEEPER
> How do you define *diversity*?
> What did you learn about others that you didn't know before playing the game?
> In what ways is your group diverse?
> How can you celebrate your individual diversity and that of your group?

ASSET CATEGORIES Commitment to Learning, Social Competencies

Adapted with permission of Kendall/Hunt Publishing from *Youth Leadership in Action* by Project Adventure.

Diversegories Game Card

SHOE SIZE

What is the:

Smallest size?

Largest size?

Number of different sizes?

DOMINANT HANDEDNESS

Number of:

Left-handed?

Right-handed?

Ambidextrous?

AGE

Youngest?

Oldest?

LANGUAGE FLUENCY

Number who speak more than one?

BIRTHPLACE

Number of different:

Towns?

States?

Countries?

OUTDOOR ADVENTURE

Number who have:

Hiked?

Biked?

Camped?

Canoed?

Been rappelling?

WORLD TRAVELER

Number of various countries visited?

Number of other states visited?

Traveled first class?

Traveled by train?

VACATION

Number who like to visit the:

Beach?

Mountains?

Relatives?

BIRTHDAYS

Number of different:

Years?

Months?

Days?

MEDIA STARS

Number who have appeared:

On the radio?

On TV?

In the newspaper?

TECHNOLOGY SAVVY

Number who have:

Developed a Web site?

Created a blog?

Surfed the internet?

Written e-mail?

POLITICAL TYPES

Number of:

Independents?

Republicans?

Democrats?

Libertarians?

DIVERSITY ABCs

TIME 15 minutes

SUPPLIES
> Index cards, each labeled with one letter of the alphabet
> Pencil (one per player)

THE GAME Give everyone one index card with a letter on it that they will "be" for the duration of the game. Instruct everyone to mingle, forming words with other "letters" of the alphabet. Ask participants to use the back of the cards to record all the words they create with others. Players who make up a word together each get the same number of points for the word.

The goal is to score as many points as possible by creating as many long words as possible. One point is scored for each letter used and one point is scored for each word created. (For example, the word "art" is worth four points, one point for each letter and one point for creating the word.) A player can shuffle the letters to form "tar" for an additional four points. Players can use abbreviations and proper nouns, and each word must contain at least three letters.

GOING DEEPER
> How many of you created five or more words? 10? 20?
> In what ways was it an advantage to hold a vowel?
  How easy or difficult was it to find partners?
> In what ways could z work with x or q work with u?
> What might vowels and consonants symbolize in this game?
  Why are they necessary to each other?
> In what ways can you connect with others who are different from you?

ASSET CATEGORIES Empowerment, Boundaries and Expectations, Commitment to Learning, Social Competencies, Positive Identity

HUMAN TREASURE HUNT

TIME 15–20 minutes

SUPPLIES
> Copies of the "Human Treasure Hunt" (one per player)
> Pens or pencils

SET UP Make copies of the "Human Treasure Hunt" sheet on page 66, or create your own. You may decide to set the number of boxes equal to the number of players. Adapt categories to fit your group. For example, for a service group, include criteria such as someone who has volunteered for an agency, led a service project, been elected to a leadership position, completed 100 or more hours of service, or written a letter to the editor.

THE GAME Players are to find another participant who fits the description in each box and ask that person to sign the box. The person whose sheet is most complete in five minutes (with a different name in each box) wins the hunt.

GOING DEEPER
> What did you learn about the others in the group? Anything surprising?
> How often do you stereotype others before getting to know them?
> How can you remember to get to know others for who they really are?

ASSET CATEGORIES Support, Social Competencies, Positive Identity

Human Treasure Hunt

FIND SOMEONE WHO...

Has visited another country	Has a birthday this month
Can tell a really funny joke	Is an only child
Has a bird, snake, reptile, mouse, or hamster as a pet	Has a tattoo
Likes the color purple	Has red hair
Has sung karaoke	Prefers baths to showers
Reads comic books	Is starting college in the fall
Is a middle child	Owns a car
Plays a musical instrument	Is the oldest child
Speaks a second language	Enjoys mystery novels

ENERGY BUILDERS

These energizers can be used to pull groups in after a break when quick energy is needed or when you want to kick off group time with a blast of intense activity. Games can be played individually or in sequence. To pair up players, ask them to mingle, introduce themselves to each other, and shake hands. On cue, players stop where they are and pair up with the last person whose hands they shook to play the first energy-builder game. Repeat the mingling and meeting as needed, encouraging people to switch partners each time. If the group has an odd number of players, one group can form a trio. Use the "Going Deeper" reflection questions at the end of "Dance Craze" on page 70 for these energizer games.

BOUNCE

TIME 5–10 minutes

THE GAME Without consulting their partners, players choose a number from one to nine; each reveals his or her number to the partner at the same time. Ask pairs to put their two numbers together. For example, if one player chooses 2 and the other 5, they can form 25 or 52. After they've determined their combined number, direct partners to stand back-to-back, lock arms, and jump up and down the number of times equivalent to their double-digit number.

SIT DOWN, STAND UP

TIME 5–10 minutes

THE GAME Tell partners to stand back-to-back and lock arms. Each pair is to sit down and then stand up without unlocking arms. Players can ask for tips if they have difficulty.

FINGER FENCING

TIME 5–10 minutes

NOTE A demonstration is helpful in leading this activity.

THE GAME Tell partners they're going to learn to finger-fence. They should stand one to two feet apart and clasp opposite hands as if preparing to arm-wrestle. Partners extend the index fingers of their clasped hands, pointing at each other, with their goal being to be the first to touch the other person. To begin the duel, partners raise their free hands above their heads and shout "en garde!" When the touch is made with their sword finger, the winner proclaims "touché!"

ONE-HANDED SHOE TIE

TIME 5–10 minutes

THE GAME Tell each player to untie his or her shoes and, in pairs, cooperate together to retie the four shoes, with each person using only one hand.

TALKING POINTS

TIME 5–10 minutes

THE GAME Announce a talking point that allows partners to get to know each other better in five to ten minutes or less. Examples include:

> Talk about a subject that makes you proud.
> Talk about an injury or illness you've had.
> Talk about your family.
> Talk about something that makes you happy.

SIGNAL SWITCH

TIME 5–10 minutes

THE GAME To begin, demonstrate three signals to players:

> Bring one hand to your brow as if looking for something.
> Fold your arms across your chest.
> Create an "L" with your arms by pointing one arm skyward and resting your elbow on the fingertips of the other hand.

Ask pairs to choose one partner to be "it." That person counts to three. On three, players form one of the three signals simultaneously. If both players make the same signal, the other person becomes "it" and starts the next count. If they make different signals, "it" stays the same and counts again.

LIFE STORY

TIME 5–10 minutes

THE GAME Give partners 30 seconds each to tell their life story to each other. Call "switch!" when time is up for the first partner and it's the other partner's turn. Afterward, ask how well each player can repeat his or her partner's story. Volunteers can share what they've learned about their partners. (You can ask the person whose story has been shared how well the other person did in retelling their story.)

NATIONAL AIR GUITAR COMPETITION

TIME 5–10 minutes

THE GAME Select 2–3 people (shyer players) to be the judges of the "National Air Guitar Competition." Ask players to find a partner and give pairs 5 minutes to create and practice an energetic air guitar routine to their favorite music. Ask volunteers to demonstrate their routines, and let judges give their ratings.

DANCE CRAZE

TIME 5–10 minutes

THE GAME Have partners work together to create a new dance step and demonstrate it to the group. You can play high-energy music as an accompaniment, although it's not essential.

GOING DEEPER
> Was the activity fun? What purpose did it serve?
> How well did you work with your partner? Others in the group?
> Did you get to know others better?
> Why is it important to have fun together?
> Why is it important to be able to work with everyone in the group?

ASSET CATEGORIES Empowerment, Social Competencies, Support

AIRPLANE AEROBICS

TIME 5 minutes

SUPPLIES
> Flip chart paper
> Marker

NOTE This is a great stretching activity for players who have been sitting a while and are in danger of falling asleep!

SET UP Draw large arrows pointing in various directions on the paper, like the following example:

THE GAME Ask players to stand throughout the room with hands stretched over their heads. Tell them to pretend they're airplanes following a flight plan and lead the group in moving their bodies in the direction of the arrows. Ask for 3 volunteers to stand in front as the pacesetters. Together, the group will call out directions as if navigating an airplane and simultaneously lean in that direction. For example, say "right" as everyone leans to the right and say "up" as everyone reaches to the sky and yells "up!" Volunteers can draw their own flight plans on the flipchart and lead the group through the plans. See how fast the group can navigate the flight plan.

GOING DEEPER
> Was the activity fun? What purpose did it serve?
> How well did you keep up with the flight plan?
> How did it feel to lead the group?
> Why is it important to have fun together?

ASSET CATEGORIES Support, Positive Values, Constructive Use of Time

Stage 3

Becoming a Team

As groups evolve and friendships bloom among participants, trust also begins to take root. You can support this process by incorporating specific team-building games into your group's agenda. Team builders require trust, cooperation, good communication, and working together. Games included in this section are perfect for practicing group skills in a safe place. Players can learn from mistakes, give and receive feedback respectfully, deepen their self-awareness, and laugh as they learn.

Tips for Leading Team-Building Games

- Keep team-building game directions simple.

- Be sensitive to cultural differences among players.
  Games should never be demeaning on any level, nor should they require group members to defend who they are.
  Remember: The goal is to build connections, not sever them!

- Use music and props to add to the fun (squishy balls to toss around the room, play dough on tables, and so on)

- Vary games to involve all personalities in the group. Some members shine when they're allowed to be creative; others excel when there's an intellectual challenge.

- Vary game types (creative, physical, dramatic, fun, or intellectual) to fit the dynamics and energy of the day. Games can act as segues to other important elements of your group agenda.

- Mix players up to avoid forming cliques and to let players interact with everyone.

- Choose games that highlight skills for participants to improve: speaking up, listening to others' opinions, becoming sensitive to differences, focusing on tasks, or exploring creativity.

- Be sure to ask "Going Deeper" reflection questions. Playing the game alone is not enough to help youth recognize and internalize the lessons that come out of the games. As conflicts or conversations arise in discussions, encourage participants to avoid negative criticism and use challenging experiences to grow stronger.

- Be quick to praise participants, but don't shy away from offering honest feedback. Be their cheerleader and their guide.

- Lead by example. Don't hold back—be as fully engaged as you ask your group to be. Energy and enthusiasm are contagious. Demonstrate by your facial reactions and body language that you enjoy being with them!

FUNNY BONES

TIME 10–15 minutes

SAFETY NOTE Ensure that you only call out connections that involve appropriate touching. Players should feel comfortable with issues of personal space.

THE GAME Ask everyone to find a partner. Call out actions that players are to follow, such as "elbow to elbow" or "knee to nose." Each player is to connect as many body parts ("funny bones") as possible with his or her partner. The challenge: Only feet can touch the ground and all previous connections must remain as players add new ones. Continue to call out new challenges until one winning pair remains.

GOING DEEPER
> What kinds of challenges do you and your friends face? How are you tackling them?
> How do you persevere in the face of an unexpected challenge?
> Do you shy away, become creative, or get competitive when faced with a challenge?

ASSET CATEGORIES Social Competencies, Constructive Use of Time

PLAYER TO PLAYER

TIME 5–15 minutes

THE GAME Have players mingle in an open area. Randomly call out various categories and then count down from 10 as players find others who share the same characteristics for a particular category. If time is up before players form a group, they're out. Ask them to help call out new categories.

SAMPLE CATEGORIES
> Left-handed, right-handed, or ambidextrous
> Number of siblings

- Number of pets
- Favorite subjects
- Favorite soft drink
- Birthplace in current hometown or other town
- Birthday month

- Hair color
- Eye color
- Sports fan
- Arts fan
- Nature lover

- Favorite movie genre
- Favorite book genre
- Favorite comic book hero
- Favorite time of day
- Favorite color

- Favorite animal
- Favorite ice cream
- Prefer to use brush, comb, or fingers to fix hair

VARIATION Once groups have formed, give players time to introduce themselves, answer questions, and get to know each other better.

GOING DEEPER
- How did you find players who shared your interests? How did it feel to be part of a group?
- Were some of the same people in your group every time? Different people in your group each time?
- Is it easy or difficult to participate in groups other than with your usual group of friends? How can you become more comfortable joining other groups?
- How do you find good friends? How does it feel to belong?
- How might you invite others to join your circle of friends?

ASSET CATEGORIES Social Competencies, Support, Boundaries and Expectations

FOUR CORNERS DASH

TIME 5–15 minutes

NOTE This game is particularly fun for energetic middle-school age youth.

THE GAME Choose someone to be the leader and stand in the middle of the room. Have players mingle in an open area. As the leader closes his or her eyes and slowly counts to 10 out loud, players have 10 seconds to dash quietly and without talking to one of the four corners of the room (talkers are out). At the count of 10, the leader points to one of the four corners and then opens his or her eyes. Everyone standing in that corner is out and will sit by the leader in the center during the next round. Once the group still actively playing narrows to 3–4 players, they must each choose a different corner. The last person left is the winner!

GOING DEEPER

> Did you have a strategy for playing this game?
> How did it feel to be out?
  When you were out, were you able to find another role?
> How do you respond to challenges, failures, and successes that may occur at random?

ASSET CATEGORIES
Constructive Use of Time, Social Competencies, Positive Identity

RAISE THE BAR

TIME 15–45 minutes

SUPPLIES
> Jump rope or twine (6–8 feet long)
> Tumbling mat (optional)

SAFETY NOTE Ask two volunteers to "spot" (watch out for) and assist players who may trip (see page 159 for supporter position requirements). Instruct players that jumping over the rope means jumping with feet and legs moving together in the same direction (this helps players avoid athletic heroics).

THE GAME Instruct two players to hold opposite ends of the rope. Start with the rope on the ground. Players line up and jump over the rope one at a time for the first round. Next round, the rope holders lift the rope slightly, keeping ends tight. Players continue to jump over the rope, and the rope holders continue to "raise the bar" with each new round. The objective is to clear the bar without touching any part of it. Players who do are out. The winner is the person who clears the rope at the highest level.

GOING DEEPER
> Who "raises the bar" (sets expectations) for you in life?
> Do those expectations encourage or frustrate you?
> How do you challenge and motivate yourself?
> What do you do when you fall short?
> In what areas do you need to "raise the bar"?
> What goals could you set today, and who could support you in reaching your goals?

ASSET CATEGORIES Boundaries and Expectations, Commitment to Learning

JUNGLE BEAT

TIME 10–20 minutes

SUPPLIES
> Blindfolds (one per player)
> 5–6 foot board on the ground (log or railroad tie, if outside; one per team of 10)

SAFETY NOTE For extra safety, ask two participants to be "spotters" in case someone begins to fall (see page 159 for supporter position requirements). Make sure open space (such as a gym or large open field) is available.

THE GAME Divide the group into smaller teams if you have more than 10 people. Set the scene for players: Your team is trapped in the jungle, and the natives have set traps to catch you. If you stay off the ground, you won't "spring" any traps and can safely reach the beach to signal for help. If one person springs a trap, the whole group must return to the start. The group must cross the "jungle" (the board) together. Reversing direction, your team must again cross the board, walking backward this time and holding hands or keeping a hand on the shoulder of the person in front of you. Before reaching the "beach," your team must make a final trek through the densest part of the jungle. Distribute blindfolds and have the group cross the board a third time. Remind players to work as a team, and give them a few minutes to plan their crossing. If necessary, appoint the first and last players to be "scouts" who can see (because they are familiar with rough jungle terrain and have survival training).

GOING DEEPER
> How did it feel to be dependent on others?
> What specific skills and attitudes did it take to succeed?
> How important was it to work together as a group?
> What would have been different about the game if players had played it solo?
> What role does trust play in succeeding as a group?

ASSET CATEGORIES
Positive Values, Social Competencies, Support, Positive Identity

LAST ONE STANDING

TIME 10–20 minutes

SUPPLIES
> One 20–25 foot rope (or several jump ropes tied together in a circle)
> 3–4 sturdy chairs

SET UP Place chairs 5–6 feet apart with chair backs facing the center of a circle on a soft surface (a mat, rug, grass, or sand). Make sure chairs are stable and the rope is long enough to form a circle around the chairs, with some slack between chairs.

SAFETY NOTE For additional safety, position extra players behind each chair in supportive spotting positions (see page 159 for supporter position requirements).

THE GAME Have each player stand on a chair facing into the circle and holding on to the rope. Tell players to stand with legs comfortably apart to allow them to be as balanced as possible. On the signal, players pull on the rope to try to unbalance the others. The only player still on a chair is the last one standing.

VARIATION Play the game on the ground. Use chalk to mark playing areas instead of using chairs to stand on. Noncompeting players can referee when players step outside the marked areas.

GOING DEEPER
> What helps you stay balanced in everyday life?
> How does planning and prioritizing help you?
> How do you protect yourself from people who try to "pull you down"?
> What helps you make healthy choices so you don't get pulled down?
> What can you learn from times you do fall?
> How can you influence your friends and family in positive ways?

ASSET CATEGORIES Constructive Use of Time, Social Competencies, Boundaries and Expectations, Positive Identity

SHRINKING SHIP

TIME 25–30 minutes

SUPPLIES

> One 8–10 foot rope (per 8–10 players)

THE GAME Form the largest possible circle with the rope (the "shrinking ship") and ask everyone to stand inside it. All feet must stay within the perimeter for at least 15 seconds. Once they've succeeded, ask if players are willing to decrease the circle size. Let them decide on the actual size. If players succeed again, continue to make the circle smaller until it's impossible for everyone to stand within it.

VARIATION Introduce environmental responsibility by using the activity to talk about population growth and diminishing resources for our "shrinking" earth.

GOING DEEPER

> In what ways did playing the game require group cooperation?
> Did your group have a plan to stay within the circle? What was it?
> How did you communicate effectively with each other?
> In what ways does the "shrinking ship" remind us of diminishing natural resources?

ASSET CATEGORIES Social Competencies, Positive Values

PASS THE CAN

TIME 10 minutes

SUPPLIES

> Large, empty coffee can

THE GAME Ask players to sit in a circle and put the coffee can on one person's foot. Tell players to pass the can around the circle using only their feet. If the can falls to the ground, they must start over.

GOING DEEPER

> In what situations is it helpful to work as a team?
> What does it take to be a supportive team?
> How do you support people around you?
> How do you ask for support from others?
> Is peer pressure easier to handle independently or in a group of positive peers?

ASSET CATEGORIES Support, Social Competencies, Commitment to Learning, Boundaries and Expectations

TAG GAMES

PREDATORS AND PREY IN THE CITY

TIME 20–30 minutes

SUPPLIES
> Blindfold

THE GAME Designate one person the "prey" and have that person sit in the middle of the playing area with a blindfold securely tied over his or her eyes—no peeking! Tell remaining players ("predators") to position themselves randomly around the prey, at least 10–15 feet away. When you give the signal, predators try as quietly as possible to sneak up on the prey. Their goal is to be the one predator who tags the prey without being caught. The prey's goal is to stop the predators by using a keen sense of hearing to detect movements and point at them to "freeze" predators in their tracks. Once frozen, predators can no longer move or make any sounds. The game ends when either a predator tags the prey or the prey freezes all predators. If a predator successfully tags the prey, she or he becomes the new prey.

GOING DEEPER
> How did it feel to be the prey?
> How can listening save you from "getting into trouble" or mishearing what others say?
> What strategies did you use as predators to tag the prey?
> What things may prey on you? How can you protect yourself from danger?
> What influences in your life can help insulate you from harm? Friends? Caring adults? Personal commitments? Attitudes? Values? Skills?
> What can you do to sharpen your own "senses" in order to protect yourself from harm?
> How can you help protect others?

ASSET CATEGORIES Social Competencies, Positive Identity, Positive Values, Commitment to Learning, Support, Empowerment

CAT AND DOG CHASE

TIME 15–30 minutes

SUPPLIES
> Boundary markers

THE GAME This game is especially appealing to younger players. Ask one player to be the dog and one player to be the stray cat. Divide remaining players into groups of 4–6 people, each with their own cat. Groups hold hands to form a protective circle around their cat. Give the dog the "go" signal to start chasing the stray cat. If the dog tags the stray cat, that cat swaps roles with the dog.

At any time, the stray cat can take refuge from the dog inside any group circle ("under the table"). When the stray cat scoots inside a circle, the sleeping cat must leave the circle and be chased by the dog. (Tell players cats are very territorial–they don't share space at all well!) For larger groups, add extra cats and dogs (two more for groups of 30). Time-outs for dogs and cats might be needed occasionally to make sure everyone who wants to can play cat and dog roles.

GOING DEEPER
> Where do you take refuge from chaos or trouble in daily life?
> Who helps protect you from trouble?
> How can you create a safe place?

ASSET CATEGORIES Empowerment, Support

GOING FOR "IT"

TIME 15–30 minutes

SUPPLIES
> 2–4 soft balls (rubber, foam, or cloth)
> Masking tape or cones

SET UP Mark sidelines approximately 40 feet apart with masking tape or cones.

THE GAME Tell players to scatter around the playing area. Throw two balls into the middle (use four balls if the group is larger than 25) for players to run and pick up. Whoever gets a ball is "it." "It" may not move when he or she has a ball, but can pivot and throw. "It" tries to hit others (avoiding heads and sensitive areas). A player who is hit must stand on the sidelines. However, once the person who hit them is also hit, the player can reenter the game. Anyone can run and pick up a ball once balls are thrown to the ground.

GOING DEEPER

> What is an "it" you want to go after?
  How will you go after the thing you value?
> In this game, you had more than one chance to be "it."
  Describe other situations where you've had a second chance
  to go after something you've wanted?
> Sometimes you realize that your "it"—the thing you pursue—
  is not what you want after all. What happens when you realize
  your "it" has changed, and you want something else?

ASSET CATEGORIES
Positive Identity, Positive Values, Commitment to Learning, Social Competencies

BLOB TAG

TIME 15–30 minutes

SUPPLIES
> Masking tape

SET UP Mark boundaries for a large play area in which players can run and move.

THE GAME Choose two pairs of players to hold hands and be "blobs." Remaining players spread throughout the play area. When you give the signal, the two blob pairs chase players while keeping their hands joined. When the blobs tag a player, that player must join the blob chain, becoming part of the blob. Play continues until all players become part of a blob chain. Once two large chains have formed, you can have them hook up into one chain and move players into the next game or activity.

GOING DEEPER

> "Blob Tag" can be a metaphor for the way people spread their influence and persuade others to join them. How can you use your personal power to influence others in positive ways?
> If you could get others to support a particular value or idea, what would it be?

ASSET CATEGORIES Empowerment, Positive Values, Positive Identity

"IT" TAG

TIME 20–30 minutes

SUPPLIES
> Masking tape

SET UP Mark boundaries for a large play area in which players can run and move.

THE GAME Tell players to scatter around the play area within the boundaries. Every player is "it." The goal is to be the last "it" standing. On the signal, players try to tag another player before being tagged themselves. Players can break a tag tie with a quick round of "Rock, Paper, Scissors." If tagged, a player is out and kneels where he or she is tagged. The last "it" standing wins.

GOING DEEPER

> If two or more players tagged each other at the same time, how difficult or easy was it to resolve the issue?
> What helps you resolve conflicts peacefully with friends and family?
> What is an "it" you try to avoid in daily life?

ASSET CATEGORIES Positive Identity, Positive Values, Social Competencies

ELBOW TAG

TIME 15–20 minutes

SAFETY NOTE Be sure to play in a large, open space free of obstacles.

THE GAME Divide the group into pairs with each pair hooked together at the elbows. Ask one pair to start the game by splitting into an "it" and a runner. Give the runner lead time to move away from "it." If "it" tags the runner, the two must switch roles. To avoid being tagged, the runner can hook elbows with a member of any other pair. When this happens, the person on the opposite end of the pair becomes the new runner trying to escape "it." The game continues until everyone is ready for a break.

GOING DEEPER

> What was the key to success in this game? Did you hook onto a player at random, or did you choose a specific player? Why or why not?

> Was it helpful or would it have been helpful if players signaled you to hook up with them?

> When you're required to do a group project, how do you choose whom to work with?

> How do you choose your friends? What signals tell you they'll be positive influences?

> What values come into play when you're deciding how you'll spend your time?

ASSET CATEGORIES
Constructive Use of Time, Boundaries and Expectations, Positive Values

AIRPLANE RELAY

TIME 5–10 minutes

SUPPLIES
> Paper
> Masking tape

NOTE There's no need to give the secret away during play, but during debriefing, ask the group if anyone thought of walking the plane from one side of the room to the other as an alternate solution to the challenge of creating a plane that travels the farthest.

SET UP Mark a starting line with the masking tape.

THE GAME Break the group into smaller teams of "airplane factories" (3–5 players each). Without talking, each team's task is to design a paper airplane that can travel the farthest distance. Only one team member may touch the airplane at a time as they each take turns creating part of the design. The airplane is passed from person to person until all have touched it at least once and the airplane is complete.

Allow each team four to five minutes to construct their paper planes. When time is up, teams signal readiness to fly their planes by pointing toward the sky. On the count of three, players point to the person they choose as their pilot (the person with the most fingers pointing their way). Pilots stand behind the starting line and launch their planes on the count of three. The team whose plane travels the farthest is the winner.

After determining the winner, give all teams another minute to adjust their designs. They can talk this time. On the count of three, pilots again launch the planes. Applaud the plane that has traveled the farthest. Repeat one more time if you desire, and if no one has picked up on the specific use of the language "the plane that travels the farthest."

GOING DEEPER
> How did your group originally plan the design for a plane that could travel a great distance?

> What strategies did you use to improve or adjust your plane?

> How well did your team work together?

> Since the challenge was to create a plane that could travel farthest, not fastest, did you think of walking the plane from one side of the room to the other? Why or why not?

> What helps you think creatively when trying to solve problems?

ASSET CATEGORIES Social Competencies, Constructive Use of Time

OVER AND UNDER

TIME 15 minutes

SUPPLIES
> Two beach balls

THE GAME Players form two parallel lines about 15 feet apart. The first player in each line passes the beach ball backward over her or his head to the next player. The next player passes the beach ball under his or her legs to the third player. Passing continues, alternating the overhead and under leg passes. The first team to successfully pass the ball through the line wins.

GOING DEEPER
> What was the secret to this game's success?

> How did your team work together to achieve the greatest efficiency in passing the ball?

> How do flexibility and cooperation help you be successful?

ASSET CATEGORIES Support, Social Competencies

SPEED RABBIT

TIME 20 minutes

THE GAME Ask players to stand in a circle around you, the game leader, in the center. Tell players they'll be performing impromptu versions of the following pantomimes in groups of three (you can also add your own):

> **RABBIT** The player hops up and down and those on either side stomp their feet.

> **ELEPHANT** The player extends his or her arms forward and flaps them up and down to simulate a trunk flapping. The other two stand side-by-side and arch their outer arms toward the tops of their heads to form an elephant ear.

> **PALM TREE** The player lifts his or her arms into the air, as do the other two, who wave them to either side like palm branches swaying in the wind.

> **JELLY** The player starts to wiggle like jelly, and the other two clasp hands around him or her to create a bowl for the jelly.

Point to a player and name one of the following animals or items: rabbit, elephant, palm tree, or jelly. The designated player and those players on either side of him or her have 5 seconds to perform the pantomime. If they're not quick enough, one of the three players replaces the leader at the center and calls out a new pantomime. If the pantomime is performed correctly within the allotted time, the leader points to a new player for the next round.

GOING DEEPER

> How difficult was it to remember and act out your pantomime in the given time?
> How do you respond to pressure? Competition? Teamwork?
> What helps you think quickly when you're under pressure?
> How might you practice thinking quickly on your feet?

ASSET CATEGORIES Support, Social Competencies, Positive Identity

ON YOUR MARK

TIME 20–30 minutes

SUPPLIES
> Coin
> Colored marker

THE GAME Have participants sit in two evenly divided lines facing each other. Ask team members to hold hands and close their eyes, except for one person at the start of each line. Place the colored marker upright at the end of the line. As the leader, sit facing both starting players and flip a coin. If the coin is tossed heads up, play can begin.

The first player in each line immediately squeezes the hand of the player next to them. The player at the end of the line whose hand is squeezed first grabs the marker, signifying a win for the round, and moves up to the start of the line to begin another round. Replace the marker for the next round. If a player accidentally starts the hand squeeze when the coin toss is tails, the opposing team advances one player to the head of the line. The goal is to rotate all players through the line and return the first player to the start of the line.

GOING DEEPER
> How did this game require you to focus and be responsible?
> Did you have to rein in an impulse to start too soon when you were the starting player?
> How do you manage your impulses when you're faced with a tempting situation?

ASSET CATEGORIES Social Competencies, Positive Values, Empowerment

DIVERSITY TOSS

TIME 10–30 minutes

SUPPLIES
> 4 beach balls
> Colored marker

NOTE This game underscores the importance of listening to others' opinions, rather than debating their merits. Answers to the more serious questions can prompt disagreement. Respectful dialogue is important.

SET UP Label two of the beach balls "F" (for first and fun) and write light-hearted, easy-to-answer questions on them, such as "What's your favorite animal?" For ideas, see questions in "It's All in the Questions" in the Appendix on page 216. Label the remaining two beach balls "S" (for second and serious) and write more difficult-to-answer questions on them, such as "What is one change you would make as President?"

THE GAME Break large groups (of 20 or more) into two smaller circles. Have players toss one of the "F" balls gently from one person to another. Whoever catches the ball reads aloud the question nearest their right thumb and answers it. Pass the ball until everyone has had the opportunity to answer a question. Players have the right to pass if they don't like a question, or they can toss the ball to themselves a limit of 3 times and choose to answer a different question.

After everyone has had a turn, collect the "F" balls and toss out the "S" balls. Toss balls until all have had the opportunity to answer questions. Remind players to respect each other's opinions.

GOING DEEPER
> How hard was it to answer the questions on the first ball? What did "F" represent? The second? What did "S" represent?
> How many of you wanted to say something when someone else was expressing his or her opinions?

> How well do you listen to others when people are talking about something that is important to you? How can you listen more effectively to others?

> How can learning to listen help minimize conflicts?

> What can you do to encourage peaceful conflict resolution?

ASSET CATEGORIES Social Competencies, Positive Values

GROUP JUGGLE

TIME 20–40 minutes

SUPPLIES
> Tennis ball
> 5–6 small soft objects

NOTE This game provides a nice segue into the next game, "Zip!"

THE GAME Ask the group to form a circle and think about the question "Who am I?" while playing the game. Go around the circle and ask everyone to say their names. Repeat the process if players don't know each other. When players know each other well, have them take on their favorite animal's name. Once names are established, explain that you'll say someone's name and then toss the ball to that person. The player is to catch the ball, call out a new name, and toss the ball to that person. If the ball drops, let the player retrieve it and continue playing. Players cannot toss the ball to the person immediately to their left or right. Ask players to try to remember the order in which they toss the ball. Play continues until all players have caught and tossed the ball. Play begins and ends with the leader.

Play a faster second round. Keep the same order. Challenge the group to catch the ball and call out names accurately each time. Repeat the pattern until there are no drops. For the final round, start the game as usual. After the first ball is in motion, pull small soft objects from your pocket. Call a player's name and toss that person the objects, one at a time, naming the objects as you toss them. Players must catch each object and name and toss them in order to the next player, as quickly as they can. Enjoy the chaos that results, and observe the order in which the objects finally come back to you!

TIP Talk about the importance of getting to know yourself and understanding your responses to various situations (including times of "think quick" stress). Self-knowledge allows people to accept themselves, reduce meaningless conflict, and become a better friend. When you know you're stressed, you can develop better focus and ask for help and support. If friends are ready to socialize, but you're studying for an exam, it's okay to say no and ask for their support. They'll be better able to accept your situation if you communicate and let them know how you deal with stress.

GOING DEEPER

> Compare this game to daily life—how do you respond to the chaos of your "to do" list and to responsibilities at school, home, in sports, and in your faith community?

> Was your response to game chaos similar to your response to pressures in life? What can be energizing or stressful about chaos?

> When you manage demands on your time, how does your response mirror part of who you are?

ASSET CATEGORIES
Social Competencies, Empowerment, Support, Positive Identity

ZIP!

TIME 10–15 minutes

SUPPLIES
> Tennis ball
> Stopwatch

THE GAME Ask players to gather in a circle. Explain that players are to pass the ball in the established order. Tell players you are stepping out to become the timekeeper. The starting player should help the group set a goal for how quickly they think they can pass the ball in the established order, starting and ending with the same person. When they're ready to begin, time players with a stopwatch and yell "stop!" when the last person has caught the ball. Call out their time.

Ask players if they want to set a new time goal. If yes, repeat the instructions verbatim and play 2-3 more rounds. Tell players they may want to be creative in meeting their timed goal. If players choose to set one final time goal, tell them the record for passing the ball in the established order, starting and ending with the same person, is 1.5 seconds. Repeat the instructions: Pass the ball in the established order, *starting and ending with the same person.*

TIP Eventually, players may realize they don't have to call names or stay in a circle. Don't rush to offer ball-passing suggestions or ideas for changing the order. Repeat the instructions, and when the group achieves a time that satisfies everyone, ask if players feel they passed the ball in the established order. If they answer yes, the game is over. Proceed to the reflection questions.

If they answer no, let players discuss what they might still do differently, and either reach consensus or repeat the activity. The game ends when everyone is satisfied that they have met the parameters of the game. If your group asks how others complete the task in 1.5 seconds, tell them one solution is to place the ball on the ground and have all step forward past the ball! Another solution is to line up and toss the ball over everyone's heads (from first player to last and back to first again).

GOING DEEPER

> What's the value of creative problem solving?
> How can thinking "outside the box" allow you to create solutions?
> What makes it easy or difficult to try new ideas?
> How do you determine what ideas are worth keeping, no matter what you're doing or where you are?
> What helps you clarify your values?
> Did "passing the ball" mean different things to members of the group? Why is it important to consider everyone's values and points of view?

ASSET CATEGORIES Social Competencies, Support, Positive Identity, Boundaries and Expectations, Positive Values

PRECIOUS TREASURE

TIME 15-20 minutes

SUPPLIES
> Beach ball

THE GAME Ask participants to sit close together on the ground. Their challenge is to toss the beach ball—their precious treasure—into the air as many times as possible without letting the ball hit the ground. Set a goal for the group to toss the ball into the air 20 times (or 50, 100, or 200 times, depending upon players' skill levels). Each person may only hit the ball with their hands, and may deliver only one hit at a time. Players can't intentionally keep the ball to themselves.

Ask players to count out loud together. Restart the count each time the ball drops. Stop the group after a few rounds and ask if they'd like to set a group goal to better their best count so far. After a few rounds, ask players if they want to plan a different strategy. If so, give them a minute to plan. Players may stop when they reach their goal, or they can set a new goal and try again.

VARIATION Introduce multiple balls into the game and have the group keep track of the number of hits for each. Players can combine the number of hits for each ball into a group score. To make this an even more lively game, ask players to stand and allow them to use heads, knees, and hands to hit the ball.

GOING DEEPER
> Did you use any particular strategies to meet the challenge?
> How did you empower everyone to participate in a meaningful way?
> When you work on group projects together, what can you do to empower as many people as possible to get involved?
> How can you be sensitive to other group members' talents, strengths, and experiences?
> What core values are your "precious treasures" that you want to protect at all costs?

ASSET CATEGORIES Social Competencies, Empowerment, Positive Values

POPCORN

TIME 10–20 minutes

SUPPLIES
> Soft foam, fabric, and/or tennis balls

THE GAME Gather players in an open area. Ask one player to throw a ball at least 10 feet into the air. Another player catches it. Assuming the ball is caught, give another ball to a third player. Both players holding balls toss them into the air at the same time, and two more players catch them. Throwers cannot catch the balls they toss, but can catch the balls others toss. With each successful toss and catch, add another ball into the mix. If anyone drops a ball, give the group time to plan a strategy to catch balls successfully, and start over with one ball. Challenge the group to see how many balls they can keep going.

GOING DEEPER
> How did the game change with the addition of each new ball?
> Did you revise any strategies as you added balls?
> Why or why not?
> How do you respond to changes in life?
> When you experience change, how can you handle each change with personal power and confidence?

ASSET CATEGORIES Social Competencies, Positive Identity, Empowerment

ELEVATION

TIME 20–30 minutes

SUPPLIES
> 5-gallon bucket
> Small, lightweight foam balls used in shipping packages
> Water (optional)

THE GAME Fill a 5-gallon bucket almost to the top with foam balls (or water, if you're outside and feeling brave!). Ask teams of 6–10 players to lie on the ground with their feet touching the bucket. Challenge the group to lift the bucket into the air and suspend it while counting to 10. If the bucket drops and the balls spill, have them fill it and try again!

GOING DEEPER
> When you heard the rules of the game, did you think they were realistic? Why or why not?
> How do you respond to high expectations others set for you?
> What did you learn about yourself or the group through this experience?
> How might you apply what you learned in this game to other challenges you face as a group?

ASSET CATEGORIES Social Competencies, Constructive Use of Time

BALLOON GAMES

You may play the following balloon games sequentially to add more challenge each time you play, or you may choose to play any one game on its own. You'll find all the "Going Deeper" questions for this section of games following "Balloon Chaos" on page 100.

BALLOON BOP

TIME 10–30 minutes

SUPPLIES
> Balloons (one per group of three, filled with air)

THE GAME   Players can lay the groundwork by blowing up and tying off the balloons. Divide players into groups of three and give each group a balloon. Have groups hold hands and keep the balloon in the air using only their clasped hands and arms. Allow 1–2 minutes to practice. If a group drops its balloon, the group is out.

ASSET CATEGORIES   Social Competencies, Positive Identity, Support

BALLOON BODY BOP

TIME 10–30 minutes

SUPPLIES
> Balloons (one per group of three, filled with air)

THE GAME   Players can lay the groundwork by blowing up and tying off the balloons. Divide players into groups of three and give each group a balloon. Have groups hold hands and keep the balloon in the air using only their clasped hands and arms. After a practice round of keeping the balloon in the air, call out a body part (e.g., heads, feet, knees, noses) that groups should use to keep the balloon aloft. Call out a new body part every 15 seconds or so. If a group drops its balloon, the group is out.

ASSET CATEGORIES   Social Competencies, Positive Identity, Support

BALLOON BODY COMBO BOP

TIME 10–30 minutes

SUPPLIES
> Balloons (one per group of three, filled with air)

THE GAME Players can lay the groundwork by blowing up and tying off the balloons. Divide players into groups of three and give each group a balloon. Without holding hands, groups try to keep the balloon bouncing from person to person, using combinations of body parts you call out (e.g., head to shoulders to knees to toes to knees to nose). Mix it up frequently or call out a combination of three shots in a row, changing every 15 seconds or so. If a group drops its balloon, the group is out.

VARIATION Want to go to the next level? After one or two rounds, have players hold hands and hit the balloon in three-hit combos without dropping the balloon or breaking the handhold. For the grand finale, yell "all body parts!" and watch the craziness. Then call "no body parts!" and see who comes up with a creative solution before the balloon drops.

ASSET CATEGORIES Social Competencies, Positive Identity, Support

BALLOON CHAOS

TIME 10–30 minutes

SUPPLIES
> Balloons (2–3 per person, plus extras, filled with air)
> Stopwatch

THE GAME Players can lay the groundwork by blowing up and tying off the balloons. Give each player a balloon and set the rest aside in a pile. On your signal, time the group as they try to keep their balloons in the air as long as possible, using only their heads and hands to hit balloons. Every few seconds, toss a new balloon into the fray. Players receive a group penalty if a balloon drops. Their goal is to juggle as many balloons possible for as long as possible without exceeding five penalties. Stop the clock at five penalties and call out their time.

Let players work on a plan for 1–2 minutes to improve their time, and then try again.

GOING DEEPER *(when the group plays one balloon game)*
> In what way was this game an individual task? A group task?
> What helped you effectively juggle the most balloons?
> What can you learn from this game about juggling team responsibilities or multiple demands in everyday life?
> In what ways do you juggle different demands on your time?
> Did planning help you in this game? How can planning help you in life?

GOING DEEPER *(when the group plays balloon games in sequence)*
> In what ways did you adapt to each new challenge?
> In what ways is it easy or difficult for you to adapt to change as an individual? As a group?
> What situations in life require quick adjustments?
> How can team members support each other through change?

ASSET CATEGORIES
Positive Values, Social Competencies, Positive Identity, Support

FIRE IN THE HOLE

TIME 5–10 minutes

SUPPLIES
> Balloons (1–2 balloons per pair, filled with air)

THE GAME Divide the group into pairs who know each other well. Have each pair face each other and place a balloon between them at chest level. At the signal, each pair calls out "fire in the hole!" to warn others of the upcoming "explosion." Players in each pair hug one other tightly, popping the balloon. If hugging facing each other is too uncomfortable, players can turn around and use their backs instead. In either case, players are not to use their hands. Discard balloon remnants.

ASSET CATEGORIES Social Competencies, Positive Identity, Support

Adapted with permission of Kendall/Hunt Publishing from *Youth Leadership in Action* by Project Adventure.

SCAVENGER HUNTS

QUICK SCAVENGER HUNT

TIME 30–45 minutes

SUPPLIES
> List of items to collect
> Pens (one per group)

SAFETY NOTE Get permission and liability waivers from parents, if needed. Contact local businesses in advance for permission to send your group onto their premises. Line up adult drivers, if necessary. For groups that don't or won't need to drive, conduct the scavenger hunt in an easily navigated area or public park. Determine boundaries in advance, and have older teens or adults on hand to help supervise groups consisting of youth under 18. You may want to assign one chaperone per group. Let players know how they can reach you in case of an emergency.

THE GAME Divide players into small groups (4–6 works well). Give players a copy of one of the sample lists (or create your own). Challenge players to find the items without buying or stealing! Groups should bring their items to the designated home base at a specific time. Set a short time limit to aid in the safety process. Announce that promptness counts: you'll deduct 30 points from their final score for every minute they're late. Review safety rules and be explicit about players staying together as a team within the designated boundaries. Send players off on the scavenger hunt.

GOING DEEPER
> What was the most difficult challenge of the scavenger hunt? Did you enjoy the challenge? Why or why not?
> What was the silliest or most fun part of the scavenger hunt?
> In what constructive ways did your group work together?
> In what ways did meeting the challenges of the scavenger hunt help you get to know your team members better? How might you continue your new friendship ties?

ASSET CATEGORIES Social Competencies, Support, Boundaries and Expectations

Scavenger Hunt I

ITEMS	POINTS
Fast-food restaurant cup	5
Box of matches	5
Printed napkin from a store or restaurant	5
Bumper sticker	10
Magnet	10
City map	15
Autograph of local leader	50
Balloon	5
Toothpick	5
Box of crayons	10
Hanger	5
Paper hat	15

Scavenger Hunt II

ITEMS	POINTS
Acorn	5
Maple Leaf	5
Compact disc	5
Lipstick tube	10
Rearview mirror air freshener	10
Street map	15
Autographed book	50
Dark chocolate candy bar	5
Keychain	5
Sheet music	10
Colored pencil	5
Club membership card	15

DIGITAL SCAVENGER HUNT

TIME 40–60 minutes

SUPPLIES
> Digital cameras (1 per group)
> List of items to find and photograph
> Pencils
> Snacks (after the hunt)

SUPPLIES FOR SLIDE SHOW (optional)
> Laptop computer
> LCD projector
> Screen or white wall
> Cables to download photos to computer
  (compatible with computer ports)
> Table

SAFETY NOTE Get permission and liability waivers from parents, if needed. Contact local businesses in advance for permission to send your group onto their premises. Line up adult drivers, if necessary. For groups that don't or won't need to drive, conduct the scavenger hunt in an easily navigated area or public park. Determine boundaries in advance, and have older teens or adults on hand to help supervise groups consisting of youth under 18. You may want to assign one chaperone per group. Let players know how they can reach you in case of an emergency.

SET UP Create a list of items for groups to photograph. To make the hunt especially interesting, turn clues into rhymes or create clues that rhyme with the sought-after items. For example, a clue might read, "Round and round she goes/Where she stops, nobody knows./Take a photo of players spinning around." The photo could be of players riding a merry-go-round or spinning in a revolving door. A mall or neighborhood where players know many of the residents makes a great place to hold the hunt. You can also use a park and relate all clues to items in nature. Determine a point system for photographed items. For example:

> *20 points*—Picture of the whole team in the window display of a store

> *30 points*—Picture of two members posing as mannequins in clothing store

Prepare the meeting place for tallying group points, sharing photos, and snacking. If you choose to download photos and hold a slide show after everyone returns, let players snack while you take care of the technological tasks. Set up a laptop computer, LCD projector, and screen at the designated meeting point to show players' fun photos in a slide-show format. Your local mall vendor or public school may allow you to use their meeting space and computer technology.

THE GAME Break the group into teams, and make sure at least one member of the group is wearing a watch. (You can split players into smaller groups of 4–6 people who don't already know one another well.) Give each team a digital camera and a list of clues or items to capture.

Set a specific time and meeting place for ending the hunt. Announce that promptness counts, as you'll deduct 20 points from their final team score for every minute they're late. Review safety rules and be explicit about players staying together as a team within the designated boundaries. Send players off on the scavenger hunt.

When players return, ask them to share their favorite pictures (most unique, interesting, funny, and so on), and let everyone tell their adventure stories. Award points and determine the winning team.

GOING DEEPER
> What was the most interesting, challenging, or exciting part of the hunt?
> In what ways did your group work together to accomplish the game goals?
> Who challenges you? How can you add the energy and enthusiasm of a scavenger hunt to your studies at school, work, and home?
> What would help you challenge yourself to make learning relevant and meaningful?

ASSET CATEGORIES
Commitment to Learning, Constructive Use of Time, Social Competencies

WORD GAMES

SPELL OFF

TIME 10–20 minutes

SUPPLIES
> 52 sheets of notebook paper (or index cards)
> Two tables
> Masking tape
> Word list

SET UP Prepare a list of 25 spelling words that use each letter only once (e.g., movie, cloud, table). Write each letter of the alphabet on a separate sheet of paper, and repeat, creating two complete sets. Mark a starting line with tape at one end of a playing area. Place two tables 15–20 feet away. Scatter one set of alphabet sheets on each table.

THE GAME Break the group into two spelling teams and have teams line up behind the starting line. Tell players each word spelled correctly earns their team a point. The game has a maximum score of 25 points. When you call out a word, each team must figure out how many letters are in the word and send that number of players racing to their table. Players find letters to form the word, distribute one letter per player, and arrange themselves in the correct order. The first team to spell the word correctly earns a point. Players return to the back of their team line and the next round begins. Keep score and continue playing through all the words on the list until the last word is spelled correctly. Tally points to determine the winning team.

GOING DEEPER
> How did players' individual strengths contribute to team success?
> Did you discover any game secrets that helped you plan and carry out your team strategy?

ASSET CATEGORIES   Commitment to Learning, Empowerment

FOUR LETTER WORDS!

TIME 10–20 minutes

SUPPLIES
> 30 sheets of paper
> (or multiples of 30 for every 15 group members)

SET UP Write each letter of the alphabet on a separate sheet of paper, and mark the four remaining sheets with a large asterisk. For groups larger than 15, create additional letter sets (per every 15 players).

THE GAME Distribute one letter to each player. Explain that sheets marked with asterisks are wildcards and can represent any letter. At your signal, ask players to find partners with whom they can spell "G-rated" four-letter words (no profanities). Once pairs form a word, have them stand together, spelling their word with letters held in front of them. Call time at one minute and ask volunteers to share their words. Play additional rounds, encouraging players to form words with new partners each time.

GOING DEEPER
> Why is it important to use G-rated words?
> What power do words have? How can words communicate what we feel, believe, think?
> How can words help us resolve conflicts peacefully and promote understanding?
> How did it feel to be a vowel? A rarely used letter? A wild card? What might that teach us about honoring people with diverse skills, backgrounds and personalities?

ASSET CATEGORIES
Constructive Use of Time, Commitment to Learning, Social Competencies

20 WORDS OR LESS

TIME 15–20 minutes

SUPPLIES
> List of nouns
> Stopwatch

SET UP Create a list of people, places, and things (e.g., desk, house, tree, shoe, glasses) divided into groups of five. A list of 20 nouns provides enough words for four rounds of the game.

THE GAME Split players into two teams and direct each team to choose a representative to come forward. Show only the representatives the list of five nouns. They're to guess how *few* descriptive words they can utter to get their teammates to name all five words on the list. (Players can use gestures or motions.) For each round, a team that correctly guesses all five words on the list earns two points. If a team guesses incorrectly, the opposing team scores a point. Continue play with the next two representatives and a new list of words.

The team earning the most points is the winner.

GOING DEEPER
> Did you take risks with guesses during the game? What were they?
> How do you decide when to take risks and when to play it safe in real life?
> In what ways does competition and stress enhance or inhibit your creativity?
> How do you support your teammates when they're under stress?

ASSET CATEGORIES Support, Social Competencies, Constructive Use of Time, Commitment to Learning

ALPHABET RACE

TIME 20 minutes

SUPPLIES
> Paper and pens
> Dictionary

THE GAME Pick any letter of the alphabet, and challenge individuals to create in 90 seconds as large a list of words as possible that start with the letter. As one player reads his or her words aloud, have everyone else mark off any of the words that are also on their own lists. Repeat with all players reading their lists aloud. The player with the largest number of words not listed by any other participant wins the round.

GOING DEEPER
> What does this game reveal about the various ways our minds work?
> Is there a learning style that comes naturally to you? How can the thinking and learning styles of others complement your own?
> What are the benefits to pushing yourself to think creatively?
> Does this game challenge you to learn more?

ASSET CATEGORIES Commitment to Learning

PARALLEL WORDS

TIME 20 minutes

THE GAME Ask players to sit in a circle and have one person start the game by saying a random word or phrase (such as peanut butter). The person to his or her right then says the first word or phrase that comes to mind (for example, jelly). Continue around the circle until all players have a chance to make a word association.

GOING DEEPER
> How does this activity reflect the power of group brainstorming and thinking?
> What helps you think quickly on your feet?
> How might this game help you with brainstorming? Creative writing? Other artistic tasks?

ASSET CATEGORIES Commitment to Learning

STORY CIRCLES

TIME 20 minutes

THE GAME Sitting in a group circle, one person offers a simple sentence to start a group story. Going around the circle, the next person adds a sentence to the story. Building from those two sentences, the third person adds a sentence. With no established outcome, the story will take many twists and turns around the circle!

GOING DEEPER

> When you heard the first few sentences, did you ever imagine the outcome of your group story?

> What is the value of group thinking versus individual thinking?

> How are individual thoughts and expressions important in group thinking?

> How can you create a safe space for individual sharing in your future teamwork?

ASSET CATEGORIES
Commitment to Learning, Social Competencies, Empowerment

GROUP POETRY

TIME 15–45 minutes

SUPPLIES
> Paper and pens
> Index cards

THE GAME Make sure each player has a piece of paper, pen, and index card. Ask them to free-write for 5–7 minutes (or give a theme, such as fun, relationships, sports, love, hobbies). When time is up, ask them to pick their favorite line or sentence and write it on an index card. After forming groups of 4–6 people, have them put all the index cards in the order they choose to create a group poem. If needed, they may add a few more sentences to provide transition. Ask groups to share their creative works out loud.

GOING DEEPER
> What was your favorite part of this game?
> What did you think of the transformation from your individual poem to a group poem?
> What are the advantages and disadvantages of group projects with many "authors"?
> Is it a good thing to collaborate? Why or why not?
> How does the final outcome of a project change when you work with others?
> What did you learn about your teammates' outlooks or values from their lines of poetry?

ASSET CATEGORIES Constructive Use of Time, Commitment to Learning, Positive Identity, Positive Values

TV REMIXES

NAME THAT TUNE

TIME 5–20 minutes

SUPPLIES
> Four noisemakers

THE GAME Divide players into four teams and give them one minute to compile a list of songs, including commercial jingles or TV show themes. Set a time limit for the game and choose one group to go first. Ask the team to hum or whistle one of the tunes on their list. The first group to "buzz" their noisemaker gets a chance to name the tune. If they guess correctly, award them one point. If they guess incorrectly, have the group that hummed identify the tune and award them a point. Rotate to the next team. Groups are not to repeat a tune—subtract one point for a repeat. The team with the most points at the end wins the game.

GOING DEEPER
> What made it easy or difficult to guess the hummed tunes?
> Talking, like humming, requires careful listening in order to be understood. In what ways does listening to melodies require listening skills that are similar to those you use when someone is speaking to you? Different listening skills?
> How can you strengthen your communication and listening skills?

ASSET CATEGORIES Constructive Use of Time, Social Competencies

EXPERT REVIEWERS

TIME 20–30 minutes

THE GAME Ask two players to volunteer as "expert reviewers" and have them face each other in front of the group. Give expert reviewers a fun topic, such as best restaurant, best book, or best movie, and assign them opposing viewpoints to defend. Avoid serious or divisive topics such as teen sex or religious preferences. Tell expert reviewers to use all their persuasive skills in one minute's time to sway the audience toward their point of view. Instead of listening to each other, reviewers should purposely talk over their partners. Call "switch!" after one minute and have reviewers argue the opposite position. After switching several times, ask listeners to declare the winner with applause. Rotate volunteers so that all have an opportunity to try their hand at being expert reviewers.

GOING DEEPER

> When "experts" argue over one another, their debate is not productive in solving problems. How can you communicate and debate more effectively?
> What does it mean to listen effectively to another person? To disagree respectfully with another person?
> How do you handle conflict? In what ways can you strengthen your listening and conflict resolution skills?

ASSET CATEGORIES
Positive Values, Social Competencies, Boundaries and Expectations

UNFAIR QUIZ SHOW

TIME 5–10 minutes

NOTE This game uses an inherently unfair design in order to make a point.

SET UP Write out a set of questions, some easy to answer and others much more difficult (see the sample list below).

THE GAME Divide players into groups of four or five, and invite two of the groups to come forward. Without telling players about the underlying bias in this game, give one group all the easy questions and give the other all the hard questions. Divide the audience into two cheering sections and alternate asking questions of the two teams. Award one point per correct answer. Periodically note the score for the two teams and use body language to express favoritism for the team with the easy question.

SAMPLE EASY QUESTIONS

> Who is the current president of the U.S.?
> What is Martin Luther King, Jr. known for?
> Five plus five equals what?
> When is Halloween?
> What's the name of your school principal?
> What are the three primary colors?

SAMPLE HARD QUESTIONS

> What is the square root of pi?
> Who are the founders of your state?
> How do you say Mother's Day in Japanese?
> What is the current national debt of the United States?
> How do you count to 10 in French and Chinese?
> Where is the Golden Gate Bridge located?

GOING DEEPER

> For the team that got the hard questions, ask: Did you feel you were treated unfairly? Explain.
> For the team that got the easy questions, ask: How did you feel about the questions you were asked?
> For both teams, ask: In what kinds of situations have you seen people treated unfairly?
> What groups of people throughout history have been treated unfairly?
> Who has responded to unfairness in ways that you admire? Why? What have they done?
> What can you do when you see someone treated unfairly?

ASSET CATEGORIES Social Competencies, Positive Values, Positive Identity

TV FAMILIES

TIME 20 minutes

SUPPLIES
> Index cards (one per player)

SET UP Think of 4–6 well-known TV family groups or cartoon groups (e.g., the Cosbys, Simpsons, Peanuts gang). List the names of each family's members on separate cards, planning enough TV family characters to allow one card per player.

THE GAME Shuffle cards and give each player one. Without telling players the names of the family groups, ask them to mingle and find the members of their TV family. When all families are reunited, have family groups prepare a song or short skit based on the TV family, or create one that reflects characters' personalities and interactions in the show.

GOING DEEPER
> How do TV families reflect real life? In what ways are their behaviors artificial and unrealistic?
> How did you find your TV family? Can random mingling sometimes create possibilities for building community?
> How can you be open to new friendships and new opportunities?
> Does acting (slipping into the role of another person) give you insights into other ways of behaving and problem solving?
> How can TV entertainment be both fun and serious?

ASSET CATEGORIES Support, Social Competencies

TRIVIA MASTERS

TIME 20–40 minutes

SUPPLIES
> Paper and pens
> Trivia game cards or books

THE GAME Break the group into an even number of smaller groups of 5–8. Have each group spend five minutes using their imaginations (or trivia resources you provide them) to compile a list of reasonable trivia questions and answers (e.g., "What is the capital of Alaska?" rather than "What is Sandra's aunt's maiden name?"). Select one group to go first as the "Trivia Masters." Select another group to be the "Challengers." The Challengers will ask the Trivia Masters their questions, one at a time. If the Trivia Masters can't answer a question, they must get on their knees and exclaim some silly phrase three times, such as "Help us, oh wise ones!" or "Ali Boo Boo!" or "Boo-yah!" Once the Trivia Masters miss three questions, the Challengers take their place as the new Trivia Masters. The game continues with each new group of Challengers until the real Trivia Masters are unveiled.

GOING DEEPER
> Which did you enjoy most: coming up with questions to ask or answering them? Explain!
> What other kinds of challenges do you like or dislike?
> How do you respond to challenges with school, friends, work, or sports?
> What subject areas are you most drawn to?
  How can you apply your strengths and interests in those areas to various careers or hobbies?

ASSET CATEGORIES Commitment to Learning, Constructive Use of Time, Boundaries and Expectations

TRIVIA ACTS

TIME 20–40 minutes

SUPPLIES
> Index cards

SET UP Determine trivia categories and words (e.g., action heroes, children's movie characters, fast-food favorites, pop songs, TV ads). Write the category and a single word on each card.

THE GAME Break the group into smaller teams of 4–5. Explain that this is a relay game in which "Charades" meets "Name That Tune." Set a time limit for the game. Have each team stand at one end of the playing area. Give teams enough elbow room to work. As leader, stand at the other end of the playing area and announce three trivia categories, which helps teams narrow their choices. Each team will send one player to you to receive a card. Players then run back to their teams and act out, hum, or whistle the word they were given. When teams correctly guess the word, they score a point. Teams send their next player to you for a new word. Keep score and determine the Trivia Acts champs when time is up.

GOING DEEPER
> Pass out compliments:
> Who surfaced as natural actors or performers in the group?
> Who was good at solving the clues and guessing the answers?
> What categories did you excel in?
> Did knowing the subject matter of a category help teams figure out a word more quickly?
> What techniques can help you remember important information?
> What strategies help you learn and remember more effectively in school? In your faith community? At home?

ASSET CATEGORIES
Commitment to Learning, Constructive Use of Time, Positive Identity

PICTURE PERFECT

TIME 10–20 minutes

SUPPLIES
> Two tables
> Two small bags of dried beans
> Index cards

SET UP Set up tables at one end of a playing area and place a bag of beans on each table. Write on note cards the names of 20 simple objects (e.g., cowboy hat, igloo, snowman) that players will create using dried beans.

THE GAME Break the group into two teams, and have them line up to the right of their table. Tell the first person in each line to run to you at the other end of the play area, where you show them the picture word. Players race back to their tables and, without talking, make a picture of the word using the dried beans. The first team to correctly guess what word the bean picture represents gets one point. If time is a concern, use a timer or stopwatch and give players one minute to make their guess. Reveal the name of the picture and continue on with the next round if teams guess incorrectly. Play continues until all pictures are completed or time runs out. Tally points and declare a Picture Perfect winner.

GOING DEEPER
> Did you prefer creating pictures with beans, or guessing what your teammates were creating? Why?
> When you work in groups, do you prefer to be "on stage" or "behind the scenes"? Why?
> How can competition stimulate personal growth?
> How do you respond to competition in real life?

ASSET CATEGORIES Commitment to Learning, Constructive Use of Time

CLAY ARTISTS

TIME 30 minutes

SUPPLIES
> Containers of clay or soft modeling dough
> 24 index cards

SET UP Create a set of two dozen index cards that list individual shapes easily represented with clay or soft modeling dough (e.g., flower, cat, pencil, bicycle, tent).

THE GAME Divide players into equal teams of 4–6. Ask teams to stand in different parts of the room at an equal distance from you. Team members will take turns sculpting simple designs as quickly as possible. Each team chooses one member to join you in the center of the room, where you secretly show them an index card. Players return quickly and silently to their tables to sculpt the image with clay or modeling dough. The first group to correctly guess the name of their artist's creation wins that round. Play continues until you run out of cards. Encourage all players to be "artists" at least once. The group that wins the most rounds wins the game.

GOING DEEPER
> Which role did you enjoy more: sculptor or problem-solver? Why?
> How did you and your teammates show respect for one another's artistic talents?
> In what ways do you respond when you must perform under pressure?

ASSET CATEGORIES
Constructive Use of Time, Empowerment, Social Competencies

CREATE-A-GAME

TIME 30–60 minutes

SUPPLIES
> Paper bags (one per team)
> Odds and ends (kitchen utensils, junk drawer items, small toys)

THE GAME Divide the group into teams of four and distribute a bag filled with the odds and ends to each team. Allow 20 minutes for each group to create a game for four players. Tell players to be creative! Pair teams together and allow time for each team to explain its game and for all to play. If time allows, let groups play several of the games.

GOING DEEPER
> What did you like or dislike about this game?
> Was it easy or difficult to create a game with the resources you were given?
> How did you work together to use everyone's ideas and insights?
> Is it possible to create something fun and valuable from limited resources?
> How do you manage limited resources in everyday life when you're problem solving?
> Which is more important—the process of creating or the end product?

ASSET CATEGORIES Social Competencies, Constructive Use of Time, Empowerment, Positive Identity

THE BIG ISSUES BOARD GAME

TIME 30–60 minutes

SUPPLIES
> Poster board and markers (one set per group)
> Chart paper
> Game tokens, such as pennies or small pebbles
> Stopwatch

THE GAME Brainstorm with the group a list of the most important issues that concern them and list on chart paper. Break the group into teams of four and give them 20 minutes to create a board game for four players that focuses on an issue of their choice. Distribute poster board, markers, and playing tokens to each team.

When time's up, have each team pair up with another team. Allow time for teams to explain their games to each other and for all to play both games. (Or game creators can take turns demonstrating their games to the group. Allow time for groups to play one or more of the games.) Keep games for further play at another time (or for use as a service project with other groups).

GOING DEEPER
> What did it mean to you to create a game about a topic you care about?
> How did you work together to use everyone's ideas and insights?
> What did you learn about yourself from this activity?
> How can you tap your personal power to make a difference around important issues?
> How might you share your game with others?

ASSET CATEGORIES Social Competencies, Constructive Use of Time, Empowerment, Positive Values, Positive Identity, Support

BUILDING BLOCKBUSTERS

TIME 10–30 minutes

SUPPLIES
> 40 slender wood game blocks
> Copies of the 40 Developmental Assets
> (download a complete list of Search Institute's
> Developmental Assets in English and Spanish from
> search-institute.org/assets/assetlists.html.

SET UP Label each block with one of the 40 Developmental Assets
(by number and name).

THE GAME Set the blocks up, tower-style, starting with a sturdy
base of four. Take turns having each person add a block and tell what
they can do to build that asset in others. Once the tower is built, have
players take turns pulling out one block at a time, anywhere in the
tower, and read aloud the asset written on it. Have them tell why that
asset is important for themselves or for youth in general.

GOING DEEPER
> What happened when you began pulling blocks away?
> *[It made it harder for the tower (or person) to stand straight
> and true. Give each player a copy of the Developmental Assets.]*
> What happened when you added blocks and built assets?
> *[It made the tower, or person, stronger and the reach higher.]*
> How can you ensure you are building assets in your life and not
> taking them away?
> What positive influences does this game remind you of in your
> own life?
> Who and what help you be the best you?
> What assets do you have that are your particular strengths?
> Which assets would you like to build in your own life?
> How do you influence others in a positive way?

ASSET CATEGORIES Positive Identity, Empowerment, Support, Boundaries and
Expectations, Constructive Use of Time, Commitment to Learning, Positive
Values, Social Competencies

SCATTER CATEGORIES

TIME 20–30 minutes

THE GAME This game works well for large groups of 20 or more. Ask everyone to stand up and listen as you call out the name of a general category, such as gum, ice cream, or cars. Players must quickly yell the name of their favorite item in the category and find all other players who share a love of that item. For example, if the category is candy bars, players form a group that includes all fans of a particular type of candy bar.

After groups have formed, ask them to shout out their sub-category to see if they have found all their group members. To get players' attention after they scatter to various groups, stay in a place where you can be easily seen and heard.

GOING DEEPER

> What surprising commonalities does your group share?
> Did you opt for a second-choice favorite because it was easier than forming your own group? If so, how does your choice relate to positive and negative peer pressure?
> What did you learn about yourself through this activity? How might you work to grow stronger?

ASSET CATEGORIES Social Competencies, Empowerment, Positive Identity

BUILD A BOAT

TIME 30–45 minutes

SUPPLIES
> One bag of drinking straws per team
> One 12- to 16-ounce filled water bottle per team
> One small roll of duct tape per team
> Large tub or basin of water

THE GAME Divide your group into smaller teams of 8–10. Explain that all the teams are entering the National Boating Competition. They have 25 minutes to construct a boat from the supplies they've been given (straws and tape). Their boats must be able to float in the tub and hold the weight of the water bottle without sinking.

Walk around, listen, and observe. Give periodic time checks and feel free to extend the time limit if teams appear to need additional time. When time is up, ask each team to point to the person they think should captain the boat.

Gather teams around the tub of water. One at a time, captains place their boats in the water to see if the boats pass the flotation test. (Boats with higher sides will float better.) Next, water bottles are placed on the boats to see whether boats can hold the weight. Announce the winning team or teams and invite them back to next year's competition.

VARIATIONS In "Build a Bridge, " teams use newspaper and duct tape to build a bridge that is tall enough for a full backpack to fit underneath and sturdy enough to hold the backpack's weight. In "Build a Tower," teams use straws and paperclips to build the tallest tower they can construct that will stand without support.

GOING DEEPER
> What examples of leadership did you observe?
> Were leaders able to encourage everyone's participation?
> Which is more important: The ability to lead or the ability to follow? Explain.

> Give an example of effective communication within your team.
> How well did your team work together? Why is it important to listen to each other?
> What compromises did your team make to implement different design ideas? Did the time limit put additional pressure on your ability to work together?

ASSET CATEGORIES
Constructive Use of Time, Social Competencies, Positive Values

HUMAN MACHINES

TIME 25–30 minutes

SUPPLIES
> Masking tape

SET UP Use tape to mark start and finish lines 15–20 feet apart.

SAFETY NOTE This activity requires open space for moving about, and members need to be comfortable with close physical proximity.

THE GAME Divide your group into teams of three. Tell each team to devise a human machine that can move from the starting line to the finish line. Only two legs and two arms of the triad may touch the ground. Once the "machine" has covered the prescribed course, the team receives a "patent" on their movement methods—no other group can duplicate their method! Only one team can proceed at a time. Give teams time to strategize at the beginning.

GOING DEEPER
> How did you develop your machine ideas? What ideas did you not use, and why?
> Was it easy or difficult to involve each team member in your machine's function?
> How did you respond if another team patented your idea before your team got to try?

ASSET CATEGORIES
Constructive Use of Time, Empowerment, Social Competencies

NATURE SCULPTURES

TIME 30 minutes

SUPPLIES
> Objects from nature
> Tape or glue
> Glue gun (optional)

THE GAME This activity works well outdoors. Ask each participant to find an object in nature (e.g., a twig, rock, or leaf) that he or she particularly likes and that represents his or her feelings toward the group. Gather players together into small groups of 8–10 to share their reasons for choosing their nature items. Ask small groups to incorporate all their objects into a team sculpture that represents each of the ideas or feelings previously brought forward. Groups can use tape or glue to join items together (or a glue gun, if you have access to an electric outlet). Have groups share their sculptures with the large group.

VARIATION Have participants find an object in nature that represents who they are and ask them to share with the group why they are drawn to that particular object.

GOING DEEPER
> How did you design your team sculpture to represent one another's thoughts and feelings?
> How well did you work together as a team?
> Did your group succeed in demonstrating respect for one another by listening to each other's show-and-tell time? Why or why not?
> In what ways do you approach being creative on your own? How is that similar or different to times when you work with others to create something?

ASSET CATEGORIES Social Competencies, Constructive Use of Time, Support

CLAY SCULPTURES

TIME 30 minutes

SUPPLIES
> Soft clay or modeling dough (small tub for each participant)

NOTE Not everyone is a natural artist, so emphasize the acceptance of stick figures and abstract creations. Create a safe environment so that everyone feels comfortable sharing his or her creativity.

THE GAME Give each participant a tub of clay or modeling dough, and ask them to fashion a sculpture in 5–7 minutes that represents a unique contribution they bring to the group. Ask everyone to walk silently around the room to view the sculptures. Then give participants an opportunity to tell the group about their own sculptures and the unique contributions they bring to the group.

VARIATION You can pose other thoughtful prompts to the group for this sculpting activity. For instance, after a service project, ask participants to sculpt one way they know they made a difference through their service. Or in the middle of group conflict, ask participants to express in their sculpture one way they think the group could work together more effectively. During group goal-setting, participants can sculpt a piece that expresses one way in which they hope to grow stronger in the next four weeks.

GOING DEEPER
> Did you find it difficult or easy to make a sculpture about yourself?
> What helps you to be more confident about your strengths and skills?
> How might you strive to increase your self-confidence? Your sense of humility?
> How can the group use individual strengths and talents during future projects?

ASSET CATEGORIES Positive Identity, Constructive Use of Time

KITCHEN CREATIONS

TIME 30 minutes

SUPPLIES
> Envelopes (one per team)
> Index cards (two per team)
> Paper clips (two per team)
> Toothpicks (four per team)
> Pencils (one per team)

SET UP Fill each envelope with two index cards, two paper clips, four toothpicks, and one pencil.

THE GAME Divide players into smaller teams of 5–6. Give each team an envelope containing supplies. Give players 10 minutes to invent and build a kitchen utensil that every household simply must have. Encourage everyone to participate in creating a crazy, unique gadget. Then give each group five more minutes to create a 60-second commercial in which all members participate in advertising their product.

VARIATION Challenge teams to create the ideal superhero on paper, describing physique, special powers, personality, missions, and special contributions.

GOING DEEPER
> In what ways did leadership in your group evolve?
> How do creative activities teach you about your own abilities?
> How can creative projects like this help build team spirit and unity?

ASSET CATEGORIES Social Competencies, Support

CARD CASTLES

TIME 30–40 minutes

SUPPLIES
> 100 small index cards (one set per team)

THE GAME Divide the group into smaller teams of 4–6 participants. Give each team a set of 100 index cards to build a castle in 20 minutes, using all the cards and working together silently.

GOING DEEPER
> How did you determine your castle design and building processes?
> In what ways did your team communicate without talking?
> Did you feel you played a meaningful role in the castle's creation? Why or why not?
> How many times did you have to restart?
  What might have helped you build more effectively?
> As you design and implement future projects together, what can you remember from this activity?

ASSET CATEGORIES
Positive Identity, Support, Empowerment, Constructive Use of Time

SONG OFF

TIME 5–15 minutes

SUPPLIES
> Paper and pens (one set per team)

THE GAME Split the group into four smaller teams and have them stand in different corners of the room or playing area. Explain that you'll give teams the same word, such as *love, blue,* or *Christmas,* and ask them to compile a list of as many songs including that word as possible within one minute. Tell them you'll point to teams one at a time to sing a song line within three seconds, using the word you gave out. Let teams know you're the song judge (recruit others if you aren't confident in your musical knowledge). Others must recognize the line from a real song (not a line composed on the spot). A group is out if they repeat another group's song or they can't think of a song within three seconds. Start the singing and let the fun begin!

VARIATION Instead of limiting players to one word, broaden their horizons and use a group of words or a theme such as nature, including songs that mention mountains, trees, and beaches (e.g., "Go Tell It on the Mountain," "For the Beauty of the Earth"), or a group of words that are related, like *rain* and *rainy*. This version may pull in the beginning listeners or nonmusical players because it broadens everyone's base of knowledge.

GOING DEEPER
> How does competition enhance performance?
> How does a creative spirit help you in leadership and teamwork?
> How does laughter build a healthy team environment?
> How can you include laughter in your teamwork?

ASSET CATEGORIES Commitment to Learning, Constructive Use of Time, Support, Social Competencies

BAG OF SKITS

TIME 20–30 minutes

SUPPLIES
> Bags (one per team)
> Small miscellaneous items (markers, toys, stuffed animals, balloons, straws, stickers)

SET UP Fill bags with miscellaneous items.

THE GAME Divide players into smaller teams of 4–6. Ask each team to develop and perform a three-minute skit using all materials in their bag.

VARIATION Choose a game show host, visiting actors, and audience members. The game show host asks the audience for a skit theme. Four actors break into pairs. Pairs work together, using props (one at a time) in a brief storyline around the theme, and compete against each other until one pair can't come up with a use of the props to fit the theme.

GOING DEEPER
> Were all ideas welcomed in your group discussions?
> Do you enjoy performing on stage or working behind the scenes?
> What strengths did you observe among your teammates?
> What strengths do you bring to group tasks?
> What helps you think creatively? What gets in the way?

ASSET CATEGORIES Constructive Use of Time, Empowerment, Social Competencies, Positive Identity

CREATE A MESSAGE

TIME 20–30 minutes

SUPPLIES
> Index cards

SET UP Write TV commercial scenarios on separate index cards. Sample story lines could include the following:

> Describe a problem the community is having, and offer a solution your group is working on or could work on to make a difference in that area.
> Describe a group project carried out by your team and identify skills used in the project.
> Describe a value that's important to your group.
> Describe a teen issue that you'd like to work on with adults in order to make a difference in your community.
> Create a promotion for the advantages of going to school and getting an education.
> Create a "teen power" promotion for actions teens are taking to make the world a better place.

THE GAME Divide your group into teams of 8–10 and give each an index card. Ask each team to create a 60-second TV commercial based on the scenario on their index card and involving all group members. Teams may also choose to write their own storyline.

GOING DEEPER
> What is important to you as a group? What issues might your group want to tackle?
> What potential goals might your group pursue, based on the announcement content?
> What did you learn about others based on their announcement?
> What commercial spots need to be produced to sell people on getting involved in the community? On healthy living?
> How can we sell students on learning and promote school as a fun place to be?

ASSET CATEGORIES Social Competencies, Empowerment

COMMERCIAL SPOTS

TIME 30–50 minutes

SUPPLIES
> Paper and pens
> Miscellaneous household or school supplies

THE GAME Split the group into smaller teams of five. Tell them auditions are being held for fresh talent to perform in TV commercials. Ask each team to choose an agent, starring actor, and writers. Give teams 20 minutes to pick the product they want to advertise and to create a promotional jingle. Agents from each group are to introduce their product and star, and stars perform the commercial. As each star performs, everyone else (the studio audience) judges the best talent, best product, and best jingle. Applause all around for everyone's creative efforts!

GOING DEEPER
> In what ways did team members each contribute to the creative process?
> Why do some commercials inspire us or convince us to buy their product?
> How do we distinguish between honest and dishonest marketing tricks?
> What is a concept or value that you would like to "sell" to others?

ASSET CATEGORIES Social Competencies, Empowerment, Commitment to Learning, Positive Identity, Positive Values

PANTOMIME PAIRS

TIME 10–25 minutes

THE GAME Divide players into pairs. Each pair determines who will mime an action, such as brushing teeth, combing hair, driving a car, or swimming, while the other person mirrors it, motion for motion. Players switch roles and practice in pairs. Invite pairs to mime and mirror their actions for the group.

VARIATION The same activity can be done with a little less structure. Don't designate a leader! Partners move slowly, eyes on each other, with easy or simple actions, trying to copy each other simultaneously. Ask pairs afterward who they thought led the pair.

GOING DEEPER

> Who are the positive role models in your everyday life? Why do you want to be like that person?

> What values do you mirror?

> Do you think others see you as a role model? Why or why not?

ASSET CATEGORIES Positive Values, Boundaries and Expectations

THE ARTIST

ARTIST OF THE DAY

TIME 15–30 minutes

THE GAME One participant (the sculptor) chooses a few other players (the clay) to form a sculpture masterpiece such as a boat, a playground, or a race car. The rest of the group tries to guess what the masterpiece represents. Rotate sculptors and clay until everyone has had a turn and a chance to express a creative vision.

GOING DEEPER
> What was your favorite part of the game? Was your favorite part illustrative of the roles you like to play in a group (e.g., leader, follower, creator, dreamer, comedian, helper)?
> In what ways did you communicate your vision for your sculpture?
> When you are in a leadership position, how do you decide how many details to give the group to complete a task? Do they need to know everything or only some of the information?

ASSET CATEGORIES
Constructive Use of Time, Positive Values, Social Competencies

BLIND DESIGN

TIME 20–30 minutes

SUPPLIES
> Paper and pencils

THE GAME Distribute paper and pencils. Ask each person to find a partner and sit back-to-back. Have one player in each pair draw a simple picture and describe it to his or her partner without naming it. Have the partner draw the same picture without seeing the original. For example, a description for a snowman might be "Draw three circles, one on top of another, growing smaller from bottom

to top." (The first artist cannot simply say "Draw a snowman!")
Let other players see both the original and revised designs. Then
have pairs swap roles.

GOING DEEPER

> How would you describe your communication style?
> What did you learn about giving and receiving directions?
> How might you become a better listener and follow directions more accurately?
> Was any information you gave distorted or misread by your partner?
> What similarities and differences are there between describing a drawing and an idea? Explain.

ASSET CATEGORIES Social Competencies, Constructive Use of Time

WHO AM I?

TIME 20 minutes

SUPPLIES

> Construction paper
> Colored markers
> Masking tape

THE GAME Give each participant a piece of paper and a marker.
Offer these instructions for creating personal posters:

1. In the middle of the page, write your name.

2. Around your name, write five action words describing your personality and style, such as *laughing, smiling,* or *serving.*

3. At the top left, write the name of one of your favorite books or movies.

4. At the top right, write the name of someone you admire.

5. At the bottom left, write one thing you like to do most (nothing electronic).

6. At the bottom right, draw a simple picture that represents what kind of work you might want to do when you grow up (stick figures are fine).

7. Below your name, write one way in which others in the group support you.

Ask players to pair up with someone they don't know well and silently read each other's notes. Next, have players mill around and find another partner for silent sharing. After everyone has had a chance to read a majority of the other players' papers, gather the group in a circle to share unique discoveries and ask any clarifying questions that come to mind. Tape personal posters on the wall as a visual reminder to players of their peer support team.

GOING DEEPER

> What was your favorite part of the activity?

> What was the hardest part for you?

> Why is it important for team members to share information about themselves with the group? In what ways is that easy or hard for you?

> How can you use some of the information you learned today?

ASSET CATEGORIES Positive Identity, Commitment to Learning, Constructive Use of Time, Social Competencies, Support

BACK-TO-BACK ART

TIME 10–30 minutes

SUPPLIES
> Paper and pens
> A few simple drawings (such as a lamp, house, flower, smiley face, and sun)

THE GAMES Break the group into two parallel lines (with a minimum of four and a maximum of 20 people per line). Players should face forward and be silent. Give a sheet of paper and a pen to the person at the head of each line. Explain that this game is an artistic variation of the gossip game.

Show the last person in each line the same simple drawing (don't let others see it) and ask them to trace the picture with their fingers on the back of the person in front of them. Each person in turn traces the picture on the back of the next person in line. The person at the head of each line draws on paper the design they felt drawn on their back.

Compare this drawing to the original drawing to see which team best communicated the original design. After the first round, have new people go to the front and back of each line and play a second round.

GOING DEEPER
> How well do you think you communicated with the next person in line?
> What are the strengths and weaknesses of nonverbal communication? Verbal communication?
> How can you make sure you communicate well with others?
> How can you listen actively to receive and understand information correctly?
> Why is effective communication so important to friendships and in working together?

ASSET CATEGORIES Constructive Use of Time, Social Competencies

Stage 4

DEEPENING TRUST

Deepening the level of trust is so vital to a group's work together that it deserves special attention and continuous cultivation. Trust takes time and is an essential dynamic of any successful team. Teams seldom grow and thrive if trust is absent. Trusting team members involves three different dimensions:

- **PHYSICAL CONFIDENCE**—Can I trust others to catch me, hold me, and keep me safe? What if it's a trick?

- **PERSONAL SPACE**—Can I allow others to get emotionally near me and into my life? What if I fail?

- **EMOTIONAL ASSUREDNESS**—Can I risk revealing my inner thoughts or looking foolish as I try new things? What if others laugh at me?

All these are valid trust issues that individuals and groups need to address and overcome. It is necessary for every team to spend time creating a safety net of trust for emotional and physical risk-taking.

A safe atmosphere allows each member to take healthy emotional risks in order to contribute to the group, discover his or her own place on the team, voice opinions, and help the team achieve a common goal successfully. Playing games that emphasize deepening trust can be positive experiences for everyone. Trust-building initiatives, in particular, can be a vehicle for individual and group successes.

Tips for Leading Trust Games

It's so important to emphasize safety tips for trust-building initiatives and to hold the group to them. Follow these tips to guide this important aspect of group building:

- Set high expectations and reinforce the boundaries as needed. Careless words can do great damage, catapulting the individual and/or team backward, if not carefully monitored. If something happens, jump in to reestablish trust as quickly as possible.

- Ensure participants' physical safety. Make sure the area is free of any objects, glass, holes in the ground, or anything else that might trip players.

- Encourage participants to stretch themselves beyond their comfort zone.

- Clearly cover the rules, safety procedures, and expectations for all trust leans.

- Make sure group members completely understand their roles.

- Make verbal contracts of agreement for involvement in the exercise, ensuring that all are paying attention and taking the exercise seriously.

- Set up, cultivate, and protect the group's trust. Be alert to team dynamics and immediately stop counterproductive behaviors, comments, or attitudes.

- Demonstrate your trust in the group. Exhibit a positive, open attitude to new experiences through your words, facial expressions, and actions.

- Allow the group time to debrief afterward and to explore new experiences, values, feelings, and discoveries.

EXPRESS YOURSELF

The following games allow players to take risks, express and clarify values, and practice questioning and articulating their beliefs.

TAKE A STAND

TIME 15–30 minutes

SUPPLIES
> Four signs labeled "Strongly Agree," "Somewhat Agree," "Somewhat Disagree," and "Strongly Disagree."
> List of values statements

SET UP Place one sign in each corner of the room.

SAFETY NOTE Players may not debate or attack other players and should listen quietly while others are talking. Choose values statements that fit the needs of the group or reflect appropriate issues that need to be examined. Watch group reactions closely, and add additional statements if an issue needs to be explored in greater depth.

THE GAME Players start in the middle of the room. As you read each values statement, players must move without talking to the sign that best represents their opinion and expresses their stand on the issue. After everyone chooses a corner, ask players to discuss for a minute or two the issue with a partner. After 1–2 minutes, ask volunteers to share with everyone why they made their decision. Listen to at least one opinion from each corner. Repeat the process for each statement.

SAMPLE VALUES STATEMENTS
> I believe the law restricting alcohol use to people 21 years and older is a good one.
> I believe curfews are important for our safety.
> I believe parents should be allowed to discipline their children any way they want.
> I feel I am getting or have received a good education.
> A top priority for me when I look for a job is whether it allows me to make a difference in the lives of others.

> If I believe a law is wrong, I am within my rights to break it.
> Making friends with people who are different from me has always been easy for me.
> If I have to choose between doing the task at hand and the feelings of my peers, I will put my peers' feelings first.
> Leadership is always easy for me—it's something I naturally do.
> I believe voting is an important part of being a good citizen.
> I believe my vote counts in shaping our future leadership.
> When it comes to making a choice between standing up for what I believe and being accepted by a group, I'll put my beliefs first.

GOING DEEPER

> Why is it important to take a stand on issues?
> What are some factors you consider when making decisions about controversial issues you face in life?
> Did you change your mind when you heard other people share why they chose a sign different from yours? Why?
> How difficult was it not to debate or argue while you listened to others?
> What can you gain from hearing others out? How can that help you learn tolerance?

ASSET CATEGORIES Positive Values, Social Competencies, Positive Identity

WHAT WOULD YOU DO IF . . . ?

TIME 30–90 minutes

SAFETY NOTE Some of the scenarios in this game may call for participants to step out of their comfort zones to defend or help people in awkward situations. Ask participants: How comfortable are you in taking a stand for the good of others?

THE GAME Divide the group into teams of 3–4. Ask small teams to discuss the following scenarios and decide what they would do in each situation. You may choose to add your own scenarios; use as many as time allows. You may want to hold a large group discussion and have each team summarize their discussions and solutions.

WHAT WOULD YOU DO IF . . .

> *One of your friends called you for advice because he went to a party instead of to the movies, as he had told his parents?* At the party, people are drinking beer and the driver who has planned to give rides home is drunk. All are scared to ride in the car and want to call their parents, but don't want their parents to be angry about their presence at the party or drinking alcohol.

> *A friend asks you to cheat on her behalf?* The class divides into groups for a group project and each student is required to rate the work and effort of each person in the group. The evaluation will play a large part in the group's overall grade. Your good friend, who did little work on the project, asks you to give her a good evaluation because the project counts as two test grades.

> *You'd like to go out with someone your best friend also likes?* Your best friend wants to ask out someone you are also interested in. The person becomes available.

> *A cashier miscounts the money you've handed him and gives you back $20 more than what is owed to you?* Both you and your friend realize the mistake immediately.

> *You'd planned for weeks to attend a big party and realize that it's the same night as your dad's birthday dinner?* Your family has made reservations to celebrate with your uncle and aunt, who are invited from out of town to join in the celebration. Your mom leaves the decision up to you.

GOING DEEPER

> What values do you call on to help you make decisions?
> Is it important to have a core set of values to guide how you make difficult decisions? Why or why not?
> How important is it to you to be a person of responsibility and integrity? To be caring or known for honesty?
> Have you encountered any situations like these in your own life? If yes, how did you deal with them, or how do you wish you had dealt with them?
> What causes or groups of people do you defend?

ASSET CATEGORIES
Positive Values, Empowerment, Social Competencies, Positive Identity

DEBATE A VIEW

TIME 20–40 minutes

SET UP Create a list of thoughtful community or national issues that can be debated by the group. This is an excellent activity to help participants learn to consider multiple viewpoints.

THE GAME Divide the group into teams of 3–4. Set the stage by framing a question or community issue and present different perspectives on the question. Teams can then choose one perspective and discuss why they feel the way they do. After a short discussion time, ask teams to debate all sides of the issue.

GOING DEEPER

> What did you learn about yourself through this activity?
> How does debating an issue affirm or change your opinions and values system?
> What was the most challenging part of this activity? The easiest part?
> Why is it important to learn to debate in a healthy way?
> How do you respond when you see an injustice or something you disagree with?

ASSET CATEGORIES Empowerment, Commitment to Learning, Positive Values

VALUES CONTINUUM

TIME 20–40 minutes

SUPPLIES

> List of "Sample Continuum Statements" below

THE GAME Set up a values continuum along one wall of a room. One end of an imaginary line represents "I strongly agree;" the other end represents "I strongly disagree." Tell participants to take a stand along the continuum at the point that best describes their views on the statements you'll read. Encourage participants to get off the fence and take a stand, one way or another, and to think about how they would defend their position.

Read one statement at a time. Give participants 1–2 minutes to discuss and clarify their viewpoints, and then call "take a stand." Once participants have decided where they'll stand, give volunteers the opportunity to explain why they chose a certain point along the continuum.

SAMPLE CONTINUUM STATEMENTS

1. I treat everybody equally.
2. I sometimes wish I were the opposite gender.
3. The world is getting better.
4. I think same-gender marriages should be legalized.
5. When I was young, life was better.

6. I'm a different person at school than I am with friends.
7. I like to be carefree.
8. People are nicer to me than I am to them.
9. I don't think anyone deserves to get AIDS.
10. It is necessary to get a college degree to lead a happy, productive life.

11. I take my stress out on others.
12. I think hitchhiking is safe.
13. I am an optimist.
14. I am happy with the direction of my life.
15. I prefer night to day.
16. I believe in a higher power.

17. I would rather be a forest than an ocean.
18. I wish I could live in my own fantasy world.
19. I am affected by my surroundings.
20. I am proud of my family's heritage.
21. I want to travel the world.

22. Certain topics make me nervous.
23. I enjoy my parents.
24. I do things to show off.
25. I think keeping a journal is a helpful thing to do.
26. I am often stereotyped.

27. I enjoy dancing.
28. Our justice system works.
29. Progress is more important than preservation.
30. Community service should be required for everyone.
31. A salesperson is just as important as a doctor.

32. Life would be okay without art.
33. People should take responsibility for themselves.
34. School uniforms are a good idea.
35. Mandatory service hours are a good idea for high school students.
36. Everyone can be a leader.
37. I am a leader.
38. I trust our local (or national or international) leaders.

GOING DEEPER

> What did you learn about your own values and viewpoints?
> Were there times you changed your mind after hearing others share their point of view? What changed your mind?
> How influential are other's views on the stands we take and on the decisions we make?
> Who or what helps shape your values?
> How can you make good values-based decisions?
> How can you be true to your personal values and still accept others whose views are different but equally passionate?

ASSET CATEGORIES Positive Values, Social Competencies, Positive Identity, Boundaries and Expectations

TWO CIRCLES

TIME 10–30 minutes

SUPPLIES
> List of "Sample Circle Questions" below

NOTE The goal of this activity is to introduce positive values to the group by prompting players to share something meaningful about themselves, meet new people, listen to stories, and build trusting relationships.

THE GAME Split the group in half and direct players to form two circles, one inside the other. Have the inner circle turn to face the outer circle and introduce themselves to their partner. Ask players to share with their partners answers to the questions you ask. Give a one-minute time limit, signaling when the other person may share. Players rotate in opposite directions, make new introductions, and discuss the next question.

SAMPLE CIRCLE QUESTIONS

1. When you were a child, who was someone you considered a good role model? Why?
2. What have you learned about respect from other cultures ?
3. What is one of your favorite ways to show others you care about them?
4. Describe a time when you felt you were being treated unfairly. What happened and how did you respond?
5. What gives your life a sense of meaning and purpose?
6. What have you learned about making big decisions?
7. Who taught you the most about the importance of trustworthiness? How did they teach you?
8. What value do you hold in high regard?
9. Which value is easiest for you to live: caring, honesty, integrity, or responsibility? Why?
10. What values do you most want to model for your friends, family, and community? Why?
11. Which value is more challenging for you to live: promoting equality or exhibiting restraint? Why?

12. Who do you respect for his or her character? Why?
13. Describe a time when it was difficult to tell the truth, but you did anyway? What happened?
14. How do you show respect to others?
15. How do you like others to show they care about you?
16. How do you show you are responsible at school? At home? In the community?
17. How can you be a good role model and positive peer influence on your friends and family?
18. What do you love to learn about?
19. What makes learning fun for you?
20. If you could visit any country or culture, which would it be and why? What would you like to learn from the people?
21. What artistic ability do you have or wish you could further develop?
22. Describe a service project of which you're proud.
23. What are you most proud of about yourself?

ASSET CATEGORIES
Positive Values, Boundaries and Expectations, Social Competencies

LIFE LINES

TIME 45 minutes

SUPPLIES
> Flip chart paper (one sheet per participant)
> Markers (one per participant)

SAFETY NOTE This is a high-risk activity that works best with small groups who have spent a lot of time together.

THE GAME Give each person a large sheet of paper and a marker, and ask them to draw a horizontal line through the center. Then give everyone 15–20 minutes to write or graphically represent high points in their lives above the line and low points below the line. Emphasize that each person can choose whatever information they want to share—there is no required area. Gather the group in a circle and ask participants to share highlights from their lifelines.

GOING DEEPER
> Why is it important to reflect upon the high and low points in your life?
> How often do you think it would be helpful to reflect on the highs and lows? Daily? Weekly? Monthly? Yearly? Explain.
> What was the hardest part about putting together your lifeline?
> How will knowing more about your teammates help you to work better together?

ASSET CATEGORIES
Support, Positive Values, Social Competencies, Positive Identity

CROSSING THE LINE

TIME 25–45 minutes

SUPPLIES
> Masking tape
> List of "Crossing the Line" statements

SET UP Place two lines of tape on the floor, allowing at least a seven-pace distance between them. If you prefer, create your own list of "Crossing the Line" statements, or use the sample statements below.

NOTE Be prepared for an emotional atmosphere if the statements you read are particularly provocative.

THE GAME Divide players into two groups and direct them to stand behind the lines, facing each other. Players silently cross the line if the statement you read applies to them. Players should notice who crosses and does not cross the line as each statement is read. After each statement, tell players to return to their original places.

At the end of the exercise, ask if players want to add any statements. Call those out as they're mentioned. Remind players that this exercise is to be done silently, and that they have the right to pass for any reason. Be sure to guide the group through "Going Deeper" reflections when you're done.

SAMPLE "CROSSING-THE-LINE" STATEMENTS
Cross the line if you are one of these or can identify with the statement:

> Are a sports fan
> Play sports
> Read a lot
> Like to go to the movies
> Are an artist

> Are female
> Are male
> Were born in this country
> Were born in another country
> Have finished high school

- ❯ Have finished college
- ❯ Work and go to school
- ❯ Love ice cream or cake
- ❯ Have worked at more than five paying jobs
- ❯ Haven't worked at a paying job

- ❯ Are religious
- ❯ Are spiritual but not religious
- ❯ Are from the south
- ❯ Are from the Midwest
- ❯ Are from the west

- ❯ Are from the northeast
- ❯ Are Native American
- ❯ Are Hispanic
- ❯ Are African-American
- ❯ Are European-American
- ❯ Are Asian-American

GOING DEEPER

- ❯ Explain that our differences mean no two people are completely alike. How did this exercise explore uniqueness and separate experiences?
- ❯ How does crossing the line from both sides help you to see that a conversation about diversity doesn't have to separate people? How can diversity bring us together and enrich our lives?
- ❯ This activity was designed to help you realize the diversity that exists among everyone in the group, beyond what you can see. What exactly is meant by diversity? *(race, where people grow up, different skills, talents, beliefs)*
- ❯ How do individual behaviors result from specific cultural experiences?
- ❯ How did it feel to cross over the line? How did it feel to remain behind?
- ❯ How do individual differences support achieving group objectives?

ASSET CATEGORIES Positive Values, Positive Identity, Social Competencies

This game and the two that follow address change and provide the opportunity for groups to deal with their "stuff" in a constructive way. Try it separately from other games to emphasize "difference." It highlights the fact that participants will be changing for the better as individuals and as a group through shared experiences.

LAST DETAIL

TIME 5–10 minutes

THE GAME Ask players to find a partner and stand back-to-back. Tell them to change three things about themselves without saying anything (for example, take off your glasses, switch your hair part, or roll up your sleeve). On cue, partners turn around to face each other and try to guess what was changed. Pairs do this three to five times, each time leaving previous changes in place.

GOING DEEPER

> In what ways do you think change can be positive or negative? Easy or difficult?

> In what ways does your behavior change, depending upon whether you're with your family or your friends and teammates?

> How might this group change over time?

> What changes might you make to work most effectively together?

> How can you be caring and respectful of others even when you disagree with them?

> (For school groups) What systems allow you to give your teachers and school feedback on what's working and what you'd like to change?

> How can you use the power of your beliefs to make your school community better?

> Change can be uncomfortable. What are ways you can help others accept changes that must occur? How can you contribute to the change you want to see?

> What action can you take each day to make others feel accepted?

ASSET CATEGORIES Empowerment, Social Competencies, Support, Boundaries and Expectations, Positive Identity

TIME 5–15 minutes

THE GAME Ask players to gather in a circle and close their eyes. Tell them they are all detectives and will be given a mystery to solve. Walk quickly around the circle and secretly tap one person, who becomes the spymaster. Make sure all eyes stay closed! Circle the group several more times so that the spymaster's identity is not given away.

Ask players to open their eyes and mingle around the room, whispering positive comments to each other, such as "You have a great laugh" or "I like the way you treat people." The spymaster should mix positive messages with the occasional "You've just been double-crossed!" and should wink at that person. Victims of the spymaster continue to mingle, pay one or two final compliments, and then lie down dramatically moaning "I've been double-crossed!" (sound effects are encouraged).

Detectives try to uncover the identity of the spymaster throughout the course of the game. When they think they know, they call out "I know the spymaster!" When players are ready to name the spymaster, they point to that person on the count of three. If they are wrong, they, too, must lie down. When the spymaster is caught, the round ends and a new one can begin, with you, the game leader, appointing a new spymaster.

GOING DEEPER

> What were some of the positive comments you heard? How did they make you feel?

> How did it feel to be double-crossed?

> How can you build each other up with positive words instead of tearing each other down?

> Was anyone wrongly accused? How did that feel?

> What can you do to make sure you don't unjustly accuse others?

> How can you handle conflict or misinformation so that you don't form wrong opinions of others and treat them unfairly?

ASSET CATEGORIES Support, Positive Values, Positive Identity

STICKY BUNS

TIME 10–20 minutes

SUPPLIES
> Balloons (one per player)
> Masking tape (one roll per team)

SET UP Mark a line with tape at one end of a playing area.

NOTE This activity can be used as lead-in to a role-play session on negative peer pressure. Players role-play "sticky" situations they want to practice responding to in a positive manner within the safety of the group.

THE GAME Break the group into pairs or teams of 4–6. Distribute one to two balloons to each player. Have players blow up, tie, and place balloons on the ground at one end of the playing area. Players go to the opposite end of the playing area and stand behind the line. Give each team a roll of masking tape. Each team picks a "sticky" player and a "driver."

On signal, teams should apply the whole roll of tape around the midsection of their "sticky" player, with the sticky side *out*. When the sticky player is covered, he or she and the driver race, wheelbarrow style, to the balloons. (If playing in pairs, one player stays behind and the sticky player crab-walks to the balloons.) The sticky player must bring back to the team as many balloons as can stick to her or his body without using any hands. The driver cannot help pick up balloons, but keeps holding the sticky player by the ankles.

Sticky players return to their team with balloons stuck to their bodies. Teammates burst the balloons and save the rings to verify the number of balloons collected by their team. Balloons popped en route by the sticky teammate don't count. Teams can stop after one round, or play multiple rounds until all balloons are collected. The team that pops the most balloons wins.

GOING DEEPER
> Think of yourself as a "sticky" magnet. How are you a force for good at school, at home, in the community, or neighborhood?

- What do you do intentionally to attract positive opportunities and friendships to your life?
- What is it about your character, values, and actions that lets others know you're a magnet for good?
- Name some sticky situations you might encounter at school or in the neighborhood. How can you avoid them or get through them in a healthy way?
- What can you do or say to help your peers when they're caught in sticky situations?

ASSET CATEGORIES Positive Values, Positive Identity, Social Competencies, Boundaries and Expectations

TIPS FOR LEADING SAFE TRUST-LEANING ACTIVITIES

Trust is a fragile thing. Developing it through trust-leaning activities can be rewarding and gratifying for all members of a group. Trust leans and other challenge initiatives are problem-solving tasks shared by the group for their mutual benefit. Done well, trust initiatives can strengthen the base of a group and help lead members to higher levels of performance and work together. Trust initiatives can deepen an individual's self-confidence and help that person develop a sense of personal power.

This second group of trust-building games in Stage 4 of group development consists of trust leans—intentional falls into the arms of supporters. It's important for game leaders to communicate to group members that participation in trust leans is optional for everyone—this is "challenge by choice." Encourage all to try, and emphasize that there should be no criticism of anyone who opts out. Trust leans should be taken *very seriously;* players are not to joke or tease at any time during trust leans. Any horsing around by group members can lead to accidental injury—skinned knees, elbows, or worse. It also harms the trustee emotionally and causes loss of trust within the group.

For safety reasons, have players remove all jewelry (including earrings), watches, or other objects on their person (think "security check" at the airport—empty pockets too) and put them in a safe place. This precaution is necessary to prevent scratches, gashes, and entanglements during trust leans and falls. If players are concerned about their eyeglasses, they can remove them before doing the trust activities.

Some individuals may be willing to try a trust lean, but need modifications to the activity. They may say "I can't wear a blindfold, but I'll try it with my eyes closed." Allow the modification, and then encourage another attempt later per the rules. After succeeding within their own comfort zone, players may be willing to stretch themselves further.

Supporter and Trustee Roles in Trust Leans

Trust leans involve two primary roles: supporters (people doing the catching) and trustees (people doing the leaning). Supporters are the protective "safety net" for trustees. They *must* give their full attention to the trustee and make sure the experience is a positive one for that person. They're bodyguards and cheerleaders rolled into one.

Trustees are the risk takers. They trust supporters to keep them safe and prevent them from getting hurt. Trustees' minds and bodies may well be on high alert, and the more difficult trust initiatives may make them feel as though they're entrusting not only their bodies, but also their lives, to other people.

Communicate clearly the following supporter and trustee positions, verbal cues, and responsibilities *before* you begin the activity:

Supporter Stance

Direct supporters to assume the supporter stance before the activity begins and then check positioning to ensure that everyone is ready. Supporters should do the following:

- Stand with fingers up, palms facing forward, extended in front of the chest, and arms bent at the elbow.

- Focus eyes and attention entirely on the person being supported.

- Place one foot slightly ahead of the other, with the strong leg in back.

- Bend knees slightly to better manage the trustee's additional weight during the fall.

- Move in the direction of the force (toward the leaning trustee), which protects both supporter and trustee when the trustee begins to fall. Allow the trustee to feel supported by the gentle touch of your hands.

- Be ready to move or catch the trustee as needed, ensuring that no one falls or is hurt.

- Stand closer to trustees if there is a large size difference between trustees and supporters (this safeguards the trust lean by minimizing the force of the impact).

Supporter Responsibility

Explain that the supporter's crucial role is that of "spotter" in the trust-leaning exercise. Review the supporter's position and responsibility *before each trust lean.* Allow time for questions or concerns. Ask if, for any reason, a supporter cannot carry out his or her job. Thank those who cannot and encourage them to cheer on their teammates or watch quietly. When all issues have been addressed, ask supporters for a pledge of commitment to stay focused, conscientious, and committed to their trustee's safety.

Trustee Stance

Direct trustees to assume the trustee stance before the activity begins and check positioning. Trustees should do the following:

- Stand with feet together.
- Cross arms firmly over chest.
- Hold body stiff and straight.

Trust Lean Cues

Supporters and trustees use specialized cues when doing trust initiatives. Go over the cues for each role, and give everyone time to practice. When the trustee is ready to begin the initiative and the support team is in their supporter stance, the trustee calls out the following:

TRUSTEE: "SUPPORTERS READY?"
SUPPORTERS: "READY!"

Supporters must maintain their stance until the trustee has completed the task safely. The trustee responds with the ready signal:

TRUSTEE: "TRUSTING!"
SUPPORTERS: "TRUST ON!"

The supporters' response signals the trustee that it is safe to proceed with the activity and that supporters are ready to do their jobs. The trustee begins the lean towards the supporters. Supporters gently catch and then set the trustee back on her or his feet, continuing to support the trustee with their hands.

SUPPORTERS: "ARE YOU ON YOUR OWN?"
TRUSTEE: "I AM ON MY OWN."

Then, and only then, can supporters drop their hands.

The following trust initiatives can be done individually or sequentially on a single occasion. For each trust lean, remind trustees and supporters of the importance of paying close attention to their responsibilities to each other.

Going Deeper

(ask after doing several of the trust leans in succession)

- Was it easier or more challenging to lean backward? Forward? Side to side? Around the circle? Be lifted up from the floor?

- Why do trust falls and leans?

- Is it easier or more challenging for people in general to trust one person? More than one person?

- Whom do you trust most?

- How can you be a person whom others trust?

- What would you need to do to develop your character and integrity?

TRUST LEANS

BACKWARD LEAN

TIME 5–30 minutes

SAFETY NOTE Review trustee and supporter "ready" positions, cues, and safety tips on pages 158–161 before beginning the trust lean.

THE GAME Ask players to pair with someone of similar size and determine who will be the supporter and the trustee. To begin the backward lean, the supporter should place one foot behind the trustee and place hands on the trustee's upper back. Follow all safety procedures. When the trustee is ready, he or she should recite the appropriate cues (see page 160) and lean backward toward the supporter's waiting hands. After one or two successful attempts, ask players to switch roles.

GOING DEEPER

> Which role did you prefer: supporter or trustee? Why?

> What did you do as a supporter to make the trustee feel safe?

> What was the role of the trustee?

> In what ways does your own safety depend on you? On others?

> What can all of us, as trustees, do to keep ourselves safe in everyday life? What skills, attitudes, behaviors, and values do we need?

> In the game, supporters were there until it was clear that trustees were on their own. Who do you rely on to support you in everyday life?

> How can you support each other when taking positive risks?

> What emotional attitudes and physical actions can you adopt to make those around you feel safe?

ASSET CATEGORIES Support, Empowerment, Positive Values, Social Competencies, Positive Identity

FORWARD LEAN

TIME 5–30 minutes

SAFETY NOTE Review trustee and supporter "ready" positions, cues, and safety tips on pages 158–161 before beginning the trust lean.

THE GAME Ask players to pair with someone of similar size and determine who will be the supporter and the trustee. To begin the forward lean, the supporter should place one foot in front of the trustee and place hands on the trustee's shoulders. Follow all safety procedures. When the trustee is ready, he or she should recite the appropriate cues and lean forward toward the supporter's waiting hands. After one or two successful attempts, ask players to switch roles.

GOING DEEPER

> Which role did you prefer: supporter or trustee? Why?

> Which lean did you prefer: backward or forward? Why?

> What did you do as a supporter to make the trustee feel safe?

> What was the role of the trustee?

> In what ways does your own safety depend on you? On others?

> What can all of us, as trustees, do to keep ourselves safe in everyday life? What skills, attitudes, behaviors, and values do we need?

> In the game, supporters were there until it was clear that trustees were on their own. Who do you rely on to support you in everyday life?

> How can you support each other when taking positive risks?

> What emotional attitudes and physical actions can you adopt to make those around you feel safe?

ASSET CATEGORIES Support, Empowerment, Positive Values, Social Competencies, Positive Identity

LEANING BOOK ENDS

TIME 5–30 minutes

SAFETY NOTE Review trustee and supporter "ready" positions, cues, and safety tips on pages 158–161 before beginning the trust lean.

THE GAME Have players team up in threes. Determine who will be the "book" and the "bookends." Ask the book to stand stiffly between the other two players with arms crossed over chest. Direct bookends to move into supporter stance and face the book's front and back. The book should lean slowly into the arms of one of the players, who catches and gently pushes him or her in the opposite direction toward the other player. Players should continue the slow back and forth movement. The "book" will gradually lean lower as each "bookend" takes a small step backward. The "book" should fall only as low as he or she is comfortable and the "bookends" are capable. Let players switch roles.

GOING DEEPER

> Which role did you prefer, book or bookends?
> Were you able to trust the bookends to hold you steady?
> What role did trust play in this activity? Support?
> How do you feel about accomplishing this task as a supporting bookend? As the book?

ASSET CATEGORIES Support, Empowerment, Positive Identity

COMPASS LEAN

TIME 5–30 minutes

SAFETY NOTE Review trustee and supporter "ready" positions, cues, and safety tips on pages 158–161 before beginning the trust lean.

THE GAME Divide the group into smaller teams of five players each. Have four players stand to the front, back, and either side of the trustee (covering north, south, east, and west on the compass). Supporters stand one foot (or less) from the trustee and gently pass him or her between them. North and South supporters pass the trustee forward and backward, and East and West supporters pass the trustee from side to side. Supporters should not pass the trustee diagonally. Prior to changing direction, supporters should set the trustee in a fully stationary, upright position. Let players switch roles.

GOING DEEPER

> How did it feel to lean in multiple directions?
> Did your trust increase, decrease, or stay the same with each lean?
> As trustee, how much control did you feel you had over the lean? As a supporter?
> How did supporters ensure the trustee felt safe?
> What do you have to pay attention to in life to ensure you aren't hurt or that you don't hurt others?
> Why is it important to pay attention to your words and actions and how they impact others?

ASSET CATEGORIES Support, Positive Identity, Empowerment

WIND IN THE WILLOWS

TIME 15–30 minutes

SAFETY NOTE Review trustee and supporter "ready" positions, cues, and safety tips on pages 158–161 before beginning the trust lean.

THE GAME Have 10–15 players form a circle and stand shoulder-to-shoulder. Ask one player to stand rigid in the center, with arms folded over the chest. As the trustee leans slowly in the direction he or she prefers, the supporters gently redirect the trustee's fall toward another part of the circle. This fall-catch-redirect sequence continues until it becomes obvious that the trustee is relaxing (but remaining rigid) and that the supporters have gained confidence in their ability to work together in handling the occasional weight shift of the trustee. Let players take turns at the center.

GOING DEEPER

> How did it feel to trust multiple people at the same time? Did it make the trust lean more or less scary? Explain.

> Did saying you would support the trustee make you pay closer attention to the trustee's safety?

> Are you trustworthy? *When others ask you to be their supporter, it requires integrity on your part and caring enough to follow through.*

> Who do you turn to for support in your life?

> When others ask you for support, in what ways do you help them?

> How do you feel now about your support team?

> How can you support each other through the program?

> How do you prefer to be supported when things get tough?

ASSET CATEGORIES
Empowerment, Support, Positive Values, Boundaries and Expectations

TRUST LIFT

TIME 5–30 minutes

SAFETY NOTE Supporters should lift with their legs bent so as not to strain their backs. Hands should go straight under the trustee's body, taking care to support the head, trunk, and legs of the trustee. Review trustee and supporter "ready" positions, cues, and safety tips on pages 158–161 before beginning the trust lift.

THE GAME Have one player lie down on the ground, body stiff, with arms crossed over the chest and eyes closed (if willing). Other players gather around and together lift the reclining trustee off the ground as high as possible. Hold the lift for a count of 10 (or longer) before slowly lowering the trustee to the ground. Switch roles.

GOING DEEPER

> What was it like to be lifted up?

> As the trustee, was it easy or difficult to trust your team to hold you steady as they picked you up?

> As a supporter, how did you work together with other supporters to accomplish the task and keep your trustee safe?

> What can you do to "lift" others up when they need help in everyday life?

> What words describe how you feel after accomplishing this task?

ASSET CATEGORIES Support, Positive Identity, Empowerment

TRUST WALK

TIME 30 minutes

SUPPLIES
> Blindfolds (one per pair)

SAFETY NOTE Review trustee and supporter safety tips on page 158 before beginning the trust walk.

THE GAME Divide participants into pairs and blindfold one person in each pair. Then have the other player guide him or her carefully around the playing area, exploring furniture and other objects in a safe manner. After 10 minutes, trade roles. Place sighted spotters throughout the area to watch for safety concerns.

VARIATIONS
> Silence the sighted or blindfolded partner.
> Have the partner groups follow one line leader, so everyone stays together.
> Try a three-person trust walk, with two sighted partners leading and caring for one blindfolded partner.

GOING DEEPER
> Was it more comfortable for you to be the sighted guide or the blindfolded trustee? Why?
> What enables people to trust others?
> What tears apart trust?
> How did you and your partner communicate?
> How do you (or might you) communicate your needs and desires to the group?
> How can you help guide others safely through difficult situations?

ASSET CATEGORIES Support, Empowerment, Social Competencies, Boundaries and Expectations, Positive Identity, Positive Values

TRUST FALL

TIME 15–45 minutes

SAFETY NOTE This is a high-risk activity. Attempt it only after a series of warm-up and team-building exercises have been done to prepare the group for this one. Review trustee and supporter "ready" positions, cues, and safety tips on pages 158–161 before beginning the trust lean.

SUPPLIES

> A platform 3–5½ feet above ground (such as a sturdy table)

THE GAME This trust fall requires a minimum of eleven players—do it only if and when a group is ready. One player stands at the end of the platform with arms crossed over the chest. Make sure there are at least ten supporters, who stand shoulder to shoulder facing each other in parallel lines. Supporters stand with arms outstretched, palms up, and alternating between each other, and legs in ready stance. Alternate players by size in the two lines to help even out abilities. Be sure bigger supporters are available to catch bigger trustees. The trustee may fall backward or forward as she or he chooses, after following the prescribed supporter and trustee statements and responses. Ask supporters to change positions in line after two catches so the same players are not catching and supporting the bulk of the weight every time. Make sure everyone has a chance to be in support positions. Remind supporters to pay special attention to the trustee's head and back, keeping those areas protected during the trust fall.

GOING DEEPER

> What did it feel like to let go and fall? Did you trust your team to catch you?
> How did you work together to keep your trustee safe and encourage him or her to feel comfortable?
> How do you help others you care about when they "fall"?
> In what other ways might this game apply to life?
> What words would describe how you feel about yourself and what you were able to do?

ASSET CATEGORIES Support, Empowerment, Positive Identity, Boundaries and Expectations, Positive Values

BOUNCE MACHINE

TIME 10–30 minutes

SAFETY NOTE Review trustee and supporter "ready" positions, cues, and safety tips on pages 158–161 before beginning the trust lean.

THE GAME Ask for a player to volunteer as the trustee. Divide the remaining players into two equal lines with supporters facing each other. Form the lines just far enough apart so that players' hands, fully extended at shoulder height, reach the wrists of the supporters opposite them in line. Ask the trustee to stand at one end of the parallel lines with his or her back facing everyone, arms interlocked, and hands holding elbows. Direct the two supporters closest to the trustee to place their hands near the trustee's waist and the next two supporters to place their hands by the trustee's shoulders.

Before beginning the backward lean into the "bounce machine," the trustee and supporters recite the trust lean cues. As the trustee falls backward into supporters' open hands, the supporters hand the trustee along the line until his or her head reaches the last two players' hands. The supporters holding the trustee's ankles lower his or her feet to the ground as everyone else assists the trustee in standing.

GOING DEEPER

> What role did trust play in this activity?
> When you were the trustee, did you trust your supporters completely? How can you increase your level of trust in others?
> What did it feel like to hear players say they would support you?
> Why is it important to take your job as a supporter seriously? How can you support each other effectively?
> What does it take to be consistently trustworthy?
> Who do you trust to support you in everyday life?
> How can you show support to others every day?

ASSET CATEGORIES
Empowerment, Support, Positive Values, Boundaries and Expectations

TANDEM STAND UP

TIME 10–20 minutes

SAFETY NOTE When the small group size increases to more than four, instruct participants *not* to interlock arms in order to avoid the possibility of shoulder dislocation. Simply have them hold hands (or maintain contact by constant touch of shoulder to shoulder).

THE GAME Ask players to find a partner of similar size. Tell them to stand with their backs facing one another and link arms at the elbows. Each pair's task is to sit down and then stand up, keeping arms linked. (Pairs who find this a challenge may ask for advice from their peers.) Next, ask players to add a third person to their team and repeat the tandem stand up. Add one more person each time, challenging players to see how many can rise together without losing contact. Remind players to switch to a handclasp when the group grows beyond four.

GOING DEEPER

> What was the key to success in this activity?
> (*Leaning your full weight on your partner.*)
> How does trust translate into effective teamwork?
> In what ways do you communicate your trust to them?
> How might you practice being more trustworthy?

ASSET CATEGORIES Social Competencies, Positive Values, Positive Identity, Boundaries and Expectations

SHERPA WALK

TIME 20 minutes

SUPPLIES
> Long rope
> Blindfolds (one per participant)
> A safe obstacle course

SET UP Create a safe indoor or outdoor obstacle course for the group, using some slight inclines or steps, if possible.

SAFETY NOTE Have additional adult spotters on hand to ensure the group's safety.

THE GAME Ask the group to choose two people to carefully guide everyone along the obstacle course (like Sherpa mountain guides on Mt. Everest in Nepal). Blindfold everyone else. Give the blindfolded players the rope to hang on to and instruct the two sighted guides to safely and slowly guide the group along the obstacle course.

GOING DEEPER
> How did you decide whom you'd choose to guide you?
> What characteristics are important in a leader?
> Did other people emerge as leaders during the obstacle course activity?
> What did the leaders do to support, protect, and guide you?
> What characteristics do you look for when you choose a mentor or guide?

ASSET CATEGORIES Boundaries and Expectations, Support, Positive Values

Stage 5

CHALLENGING THE TEAM

This stage of group development separates the little league from the major league. It's fair to expect that a group will deal with some "storming" or conflict as it grapples with issues presented in these more difficult team challenges: "Who leads?" "How do we handle stress?" These are the issues that will test the mettle of the group. Teams that can successfully solve intellectual and physical problems and resolve conflict will develop solid skills in cooperation, leadership, risk taking, and decision making.

Various individual strengths and leadership skills emerge as different styles and skills are called for. The crucial question for teams is: Will team members share leadership? And if they do so, emerging as a team that performs and works well together, will they *continue* to maintain their successes and hold each other accountable? Accountability is a key component of successful teams and is the highest level of responsibility for teams that work well together.

Tips for Leading Problem-Solving Initiative Games

Keep these tips in mind when you lead groups in problem-solving initiatives:

- When you give players directions for games in this section, they may at first be confused. Let them struggle with how to solve the problem or challenge at hand. Resist immediately jumping in to help. Know that struggle is part of the process; given time, players will probably come up with the solutions themselves. They may experience frustration, confusion, and finally "ah ha!" moments as solutions unfold.

- Cheerlead and encourage, but allow players to fail, get back up, and try again. Lead by example and hold players accountable for themselves.

- Choose activities you understand clearly and are comfortable leading.

- Consider your group's physical limitations, their group stability, and their readiness. Ensure involvement possibilities for all members of the team. For example, if a player uses a wheelchair, create a role that allows an active contribution to the overall success of the group.

- Ensure the physical safety of the playing area and enforce safe boundaries.

- Clearly cover rules and safety procedures—make rules simple and concise. Ensure that everyone understands the rules before beginning.

- Be patient—present the challenge, and let the *group* work through the initiative.

- If the group has 20 or more members, break them into smaller teams with a *game leader for each group.*

- Always allow time to process "Going Deeper" reflection questions after completing the initiatives.

- Celebrate breakthroughs and teamwork.

MAGICAL STONES

TIME 30–60 minutes

SUPPLIES
> Masking tape
> Open space (inside or outside)

SET UP Mark the starting line with a straight line of masking tape. Pace off seven big steps and place another strip of tape parallel to the first strip. Make sure the playing area is free of obstructions (roots, holes, furniture, or walls).

THE STORY Your group is visiting the School of Magic and competing against other teams in the Magical Stones competition. You are at the top of a mountain and have been given only seven magic stones to help you cross the valley below to the mountain on the other side. Teammates must help each other cross the open space together and have 35 minutes to complete the task. (Adjust the timeframe and give players 5–10 minutes to plan their strategy, if needed.)

THE GAME Gather the group behind the starting line. For large groups, divide players into teams of eight or nine. The team's challenge is to move from the starting line across the dangerous middle space to the end tape on the far side, using the seven magic stones. Instruct the group to begin after they listen closely to the rules.

Magical stones (imaginary points on the floor) completely line the space between the boundaries. A magic stone is activated when any body part touches it (a touch activates one stone). Any spot on a person's body (foot, elbow, hand, knee, rear end) that activates a magic stone is counted as one of the team's seven stones. (If someone lies down across the space, they use up all seven team points, leaving none to help others get across the space.) A magical stone stays activated as long as a body part is in contact with it.

The magical stone disappears when contact with a body part ends. (If someone rotates a foot or falls backward, they use up the one stone and activate another. This exercise calls for steadiness.)

No "flying" (leaping or throwing players) is allowed. Seven magic stones and good teamwork will get the whole group across safely. (No one should suddenly have to become an acrobat to accomplish this feat!)

NOTE You'll probably have to remind players of the rules and keep close count of the number of steps they use. Many participants plant a foot and then move it, activating at least two magic stones. Make them aware of what they're doing, and if players use their seven points, have them try again.

At some point, players realize they need to step on each others' feet to complete the challenge successfully. Caution them to take off their shoes (especially heels). But let them come up with the idea to cross by stepping on each others' feet, and simply say they might want to try it barefoot.

This initiative tends to become frustrating. Cheer them on. Remind players that the task is doable and the answer lies within them, working together as a team.

SOLUTION This initiative can be solved without presenting undue risk to anyone. Players will probably think individually at first. They may try to leap the distance and use up one magical stone in a single jump. Remind them that it works for the individual but leaves only six points of contact for the rest of the team.

Some may want to throw teammates across the void or carry players on their backs. Remind them that this activity, if solved carefully, will not harm anyone (don't let them throw players across). Depending on the size of the players, you might let them try to carry someone on their back, but be sure to count the number of steps they use—that will help them see that the action causes them to take too many steps.

To successfully solve this initiative, someone usually keeps a foot planted on the safe side of the tape (no points wasted) and steps out to plant the other foot on a magical stone (or jumps into the middle, establishing two points, close enough to land so that others can step from land onto their feet). A second teammate walks across the feet of the first player and sets up two new points. The third teammate walks across the three points and establishes two more points (five points in the middle so far). A fourth person walks across and establishes the last two points (depending on their stretch, the fourth person may establish the sixth point in the middle and place the other foot on the land side of the far boundary, leaving one magical stone for a "mess up" somewhere along the way).

Once the human bridge is in place, players can walk across, holding on to their teammates. The last part of the bridge moves across until everyone reaches safety on the other side. Generally, the human bridge ends up as a straight line (a little more difficult to cross without several missteps), or every other person faces the other (with feet also facing each other), making it easier to support players as they go across.

GOING DEEPER

> What happened in this initiative?
> Did it take the entire team to accomplish the initiative? How?
> Give an example of effective communication in this activity.
> Did everyone feel they had a voice in this activity?
  Why or why not?
> What different methods of communication did your team use?
> What suggestions were acted upon?
  What suggestions were ignored?
> How did it feel to be heard when you made a suggestion?
> Did anything interfere with your ability to listen to each other?
> What leadership roles did people take during this activity?
> Who supported each other and made sure everyone
  was included?
> Did you follow the leader even if you weren't sure the idea
  would work? Why?
> What did it feel like to accomplish the initiative?

ASSET CATEGORIES Social Competencies, Positive Identity, Positive Values, Boundaries and Expectations, Empowerment

BLIND COUNT

TIME 10–20 minutes

THE GAME Ask players to spread out in an open area and face in various directions with eyes closed. The group goal is to count aloud to 10, one person at a time, without anyone reciting two numbers in a row or counting at the same time as another player. If either happens, the group must start over. No talking (except to count), no planning, and no peeking!

GOING DEEPER

> Did this activity frustrate you? Why or why not?

> In this game, players faced two handicaps: you couldn't see and you couldn't plan a strategy. Are there situations in life in which people cope with multiple disadvantages on a daily basis? What are they? What can you do to empower or help them to overcome challenges?

> In what ways do the frustrations of this game make you more empathetic and compassionate toward those who face disadvantages daily?

> Describe situations where you felt you were working in the "dark."

> How do you keep your personal power strong when you face tough situations?

ASSET CATEGORIES
Positive Identity, Positive Values, Empowerment, Social Competencies

ICE CREAM SUNDAE CHALLENGE

TIME 30 minutes

SUPPLIES
> A long 2 x 4 beam (10–12 feet long)
> Several tumbling mats

SET UP Place the beam on the ground (or raised no more than 1½ feet) and over several tumbling mats in a safe, open playing space.

THE GAME Divide the group into two teams. Name them "chocolate" and "vanilla," and have them start at opposite ends of the beam. Tell teams to create an imaginary ice cream sundae by alternating chocolate and vanilla team members standing on the beam. Facing the center, each player must move along the beam toward the opposite end without touching the ground. Agree that if a player steps or falls off the beam, he or she does not pull off the whole group. Set a time limit and deduct penalty points for players who fall off. For extra challenge, have teams play silently!

GOING DEEPER
> What strategy did your team use to get from one end to the other?
> How can you support each another in similar fashion in future activities?
> What was the most frustrating moment of this activity?
> In what ways did your team overcome frustration?
> How can you overcome frustrations in future activities?

ASSET CATEGORIES Social Competencies, Empowerment

SNOWSHOES

TIME 30–40 minutes

SUPPLIES
- Two 4" x 4" beams (no more than 12 feet long)
- 24 four-foot ropes

SET UP Insert 12 four-foot ropes through 12 holes drilled horizontally in each beam at one-foot intervals. Tie the ropes into loops. Place beams parallel and about two feet apart. Mark starting and ending boundary lines about 25 feet apart.

THE STORY Set the scene: "Your airplane has crashed in the Himalayan Mountains, and your only route to civilization lies across 12-foot snowdrifts. Special snowshoes will help you walk, but you must all work together. Watch out for the dreaded snow elves, who steal any ropes and feet that touch the snow!"

THE GAME The group's task is to lift and move the beams while holding on to the ropes by placing one foot on each beam. Instruct players who start to fall to let go of the ropes and step off the beams to avoid causing others to fall. If a player falls off, the entire group returns to the starting point. The object is for the entire group to move forward to the ending line while holding the ropes and without falling once.

VARIATION If a player falls, have that person return to his place, facing backward. You can also have the entire group move the beams while facing backward.

GOING DEEPER
- What did you learn during this activity that you can apply to future team activities?
- In what ways was it easy or difficult to rely on others to succeed?
- What did it take to move together as one team?
- How well did you communicate?

ASSET CATEGORIES
Support, Empowerment, Boundaries and Expectations, Social Competencies

CHANGE OVER

TIME 25–35 minutes

SUPPLIES
> An old tarp or sheet that can be walked on (large enough to fit team members standing together)

SAFETY NOTE Players are not allowed to stand on each other's shoulders.

THE GAME Ask the team to stand together on the tarp. Without stepping off the tarp, players must turn the tarp completely over and remain standing on the tarp the entire time. As players problem-solve, intervene if they explore any unsafe solutions (such as sitting on shoulders).

GOING DEEPER
> What strategies did you consider to solve this puzzle?
> How effectively did you and your teammates work together? What could you have done differently?
> Are there any ways you'd like to see the group change?
> What would you like to change in your life?

ASSET CATEGORIES
Support, Boundaries and Expectations, Social Competencies, Positive Identity

ALL ABOARD

TIME 20–30 minutes

SUPPLIES
> Milk crate (grocery stores and dairies may have extras)

SAFETY NOTE Be aware of differences in team members' strength and body sizes. Instruct players not to lift, support, or be supported in ways that make them uncomfortable. Players should not attempt any solution that doesn't incorporate an adequate number of spotters to ensure safety.

THE STORY Set the scene: "A toxic slime is quickly approaching your island! You have to get everyone to safety at the top of the mountain for a helicopter rescue."

THE GAME See how many team members can balance on the milk crate for five seconds. Keep challenging the team to add more members. Players on the milk crate cannot touch the ground with any part of their bodies.

GOING DEEPER

> How did it feel to have others invading your personal space?
> What was your biggest challenge and how did you overcome it?
> What made you most uncomfortable during this activity?
> How can you apply or relate this activity to working within your team?
> What were some of your most creative solutions to the problem?
> Did your team expectations change throughout the process?

ASSET CATEGORIES
Social Competencies, Boundaries and Expectations, Empowerment

THE CHOCOLATE FACTORY

TIME 30 minutes

SUPPLIES

> Miniature candy bars
> Paper plates (equal to the group number minus one)
> Masking tape

SET UP Mark the starting line of the play area with tape. Pace off steps equal to the number of players plus two and mark the ending line with tape.

THE STORY Set the scene: Welcome to the Chocolate Factory! You must cross the steaming vat of hot chocolate in order to visit the chocolate factory on the other side. Beware—if you lose your balance and fall into the vat of hot chocolate, you become part of the candy bar! If everyone crosses safely, chocolate candy bars are your reward.

THE GAME Gather everyone at the starting line and distribute a paper plate ("marshmallow") to each player. Players must use their marshmallows to float across the hot chocolate. Part of their body must touch a marshmallow (theirs or someone else's) at all times (otherwise, the marshmallow will melt). Marshmallows can be passed from player to player in the vat of chocolate. More than one player at a time can touch or share a marshmallow.

When a player loses his or her balance and falls, the whole team must return to the start and begin again. If the whole group crosses safely, reward them with chocolate bars.

VARIATION To add to the fun, give the group only 20 minutes to complete the task.

GOING DEEPER
> How did the team make group decisions that allowed you all to complete this activity?
> What strategies worked effectively?
> How well did the group listen to each other's ideas?
> What did you like or not like about how you worked together?
> Give an example of team work in this game.
> Why is it important to show respect for others' ideas, even if you don't agree with them?

ASSET CATEGORIES
Empowerment, Social Competencies, Boundaries and Expectations

GUIDING LIGHTS

TIME 20–30 minutes

SUPPLIES
> 2–3 blindfolds
> Masking tape

SET UP Use tape to mark starting and ending lines within a play area large enough for the team to create a human obstacle course.

THE STORY Set the scene: A ship at sea is trying to sail safely into port. The ship must navigate a treacherous harbor filled with rocks. A lighthouse will give signals to guide the ship to safety.

THE GAME Choose one player to be the "ship" and another player to lead the ship away from the playing area so they can't hear or see the other players. Select one player to be the "guiding light" (lighthouse) and two more players to be "conflicting lights." Direct all three lights to stand side by side at the far end of the obstacle course. Other players should kneel, sit, or lie on the ground to form the obstacle course within the play area. These players are the "rocks" in the harbor and must stay quiet so they don't give away their positions. Bring the blindfolded ship back to the start of the obstacle course and allow the returning player who blindfolded the ship to assume a position within the obstacle course.

The guiding light's job is to safely guide the blindfolded ship through the harbor. The guiding light and conflicting lights may talk to the ship from their stationary positions at the end of the obstacle course, but cannot touch the ship in any way. Conflicting lights try to steer the ship into obstacles and convince the ship they are the true guiding lights. They give the ship correct advice at times, mingled with incorrect information (even apologizing for their mistakes and further attempting to deceive the ship). The guiding light must counter with correct directions. Set a time limit for the lighthouse to guide the ship to harbor, which adds to the chaos and frantic feeling of the event. Play out the scenario, and then allow others to assume the lead roles.

GOING DEEPER

> What was it like to play the part of a conflicting or guiding light?
> If you played the role of the ship, how did you determine which voice to trust?
> In what ways was it difficult or easy to determine whom to trust?
> How difficult or easy was it to lead the "ship" astray? What strategy did you use to gain the ship's trust?
> How do you decide which voices to listen to?
> How do you distinguish between voices that may harm you and those that may help you?
> What values can serve as your compass in deciding which situations you should resist and which are okay?

ASSET CATEGORIES Boundaries and Expectations, Social Competencies, Positive Identity, Positive Values, Empowerment

THE WINDING ROAD

TIME 20–40 minutes

SUPPLIES

> Objects to create an obstacle course
> (chairs, paper, baseball bases, balls, balloons, squishy toys—items that won't hurt if bumped into or stepped on)
> Blindfolds—one per pair of players
> Cones or masking tape

NOTE "The Winding Road" can be played alone or as one in a series. Play the two variations that follow it in sequence, building one upon the other to add depth to the group's experience. You can change the obstacle course each time to add difficulty and keep group interest high.

SET UP Set up an obstacle course area using cones or tape to outline the Winding Road, and place obstacles inside the boundaries. Leave enough space between obstacles for players to be able to walk around them.

THE GAME Split players into pairs. Let each pair determine the "guide" and the "traveler." Blindfold travelers. Each guide leads their traveler to one of the edges of the Winding Road. Guides step away from their travelers and go to the side opposite their travelers. Guides attempt to lead their travelers along the Winding Road without guiding them onto or into any of the obstacles or other travelers. Guides cannot physically touch their travelers, but can talk to them. Have guides keep track of how many times their travelers run into or touch obstacles.

For additional interest, you can challenge each pair to determine how many "touches" they will allow themselves (with the goal being to avoid touching any of the obstacles). Play again, having partners switch roles.

VARIATIONS If travelers touch an obstacle, have them start over, or have travelers go through the obstacle course one at a time.

GOING DEEPER

> How difficult was it to hear your guide when so many voices were guiding others at the same time?

> As a guide, how did you support your partner through the challenge?

> As a traveler, how did you feel as you relied on your partner's support?

> When have you positively guided someone through a tricky situation? What happened?

> Who supports and guides you through tricky spots?

> How can you thank that person for being a positive influence in your life?

> What do you do when you hit snags in everyday life, at school, work, or home?

> How do you overcome obstacles and move on toward your goal?

> What goals keep you focused and moving forward?

> How can you actively support each other as you work together in the future?

ASSET CATEGORIES Positive Identity, Support, Boundaries and Expectations, Social Competencies, Empowerment, Positive Values

THE WINDING ROAD: CROSSING THE PIT OF DESPAIR

TIME 20–40 minutes

SUPPLIES
> Markers
> Balloons
> Blindfolds
> Objects to create an obstacle course (see "The Winding Road")
> Cones or masking tape

SET UP Set up an obstacle course area using cones or tape to outline the Winding Road, and place obstacles inside the boundaries. Leave enough space between obstacles for players to be able to walk around them.

THE GAME This game is set up like the preceding game, except that all players blow up and tie off balloons and write on their balloon one or more dashed hopes, despairs, or worries they have about life. Players should pair up. Let each pair determine the guide and the traveler. Travelers should be blindfolded, and guides should place travelers' balloons at random within the obstacle course (the "Pit of Despair"— not a fun place to be).

Remind guides not to place balloons at the edge of the obstacle course. Make it challenging! Guides verbally lead their travelers through the pit to retrieve their balloons of worry and then guide them to safety. Once out of the Pit, travelers can take off their blindfolds and burst their balloons (destroy their worries once and forever)! Switch roles and play again.

GOING DEEPER

If you play this version as a stand-alone game, see additional questions on page 186.

> How is the Pit of Despair a metaphor for life?
> How were you able to cross the Pit of Despair?
> How did it feel to destroy your worries, despair, and dashed hopes and let them go?
> What one thing can you do to deal creatively with your real life worries and despairs?

> Who or what can help you deal with them?

> What tips could you apply from this game to real life obstacles?

ASSET CATEGORIES   Positive Identity, Support, Boundaries and Expectations, Social Competencies, Positive Values, Empowerment

THE WINDING ROAD: CROSSING THE SEA OF HOPE

TIME 20–40 minutes

SUPPLIES
> Index cards (3–5 per player)
> Pens or pencils
> Blindfolds and objects to create an obstacle course (see "The Winding Road")
> Cones or masking tape

SET UP Mark off an obstacle course area using cones or tape to outline the Winding Road. Place obstacles inside the boundaries. Leave enough space between obstacles for players to be able to walk around them.

THE GAME This game is similar to the original Winding Road except that this time, begin by asking the group what gives them hope for a positive future and helps guide them through life. After some discussion, ask how setting goals can help direct their choices and behaviors, enabling them to have a good life. Have players write on an index card the hopes and goals they have for themselves—at school, for life in general, or outside school. Their goals may relate to their family, their career, or their relationships.

Players should pair up. Let pairs determine the traveler and the guide. Travelers should be blindfolded, and guides should place the goal cards at random within the obstacle course (the Sea of Hope). Remind guides not to place goal cards within easy reach, because people do have to work for their goals! Guides verbally lead their travelers through the Sea of Hope to their goals. Once successfully through the Sea of Hope, travelers should hang on to their goals for later discussion. Have travelers and guides switch roles.

When all players have crossed the Sea of Hope, gather players in a circle. Ask for volunteers to share their hopes for a positive future and to share one of their goals. After each person shares their hopes and goals, the group can positively affirm them with a supportive cheer.

GOING DEEPER

If you're playing this version as a stand-alone game, see additional questions on page 186.

> Did everyone reach their goals and hopes and get through the Sea of Hope? Did everyone succeed? How did it feel?

> How was skirting obstacles in the Sea of Hope like navigating real life? Do obstacles get in your way when you work toward goals?

> Do obstacles have to stop you from reaching for what you want in life?

> Was it easy or hard to articulate your hopes and goals?

> Did you hear others mention hopes or goals that you'd like to adopt for yourself? What are they?

> Is it easy or difficult to picture a positive future for yourself? Why or why not?

> How can you keep yourself focused on hope and steer clear of obstacles? Are there people, attitudes, skills, or activities that can help you?

> What resources can you tap into to help you stay your course?

ASSET CATEGORIES Positive Identity, Support, Boundaries and Expectations, Social Competencies, Positive Values, Empowerment, Commitment to Learning

PERFECT SQUARE

TIME 20–25 minutes

SUPPLIES
> A long rope or string
> Blindfold (one per player)
> Large, flat playing space

SAFETY TIP Designate a few supporters (participants or adult leaders) to watch for potential mishaps, such as tripping or running into obstacles.

THE GAME Blindfold all participants and have them hold on to the rope. Tell them they have 15 minutes to work together to form a perfect square. Every participant must maintain contact with the rope at all times until they have completed the task. No one may remove his or her blindfold until the activity is completed. When everyone in the group thinks the group has formed the square, they should stand in place, drop the rope, and remove their blindfolds.

GOING DEEPER
> Did you feel you had a meaningful role to play?
> What was challenging in this game? Easy?
> How did your group develop a plan?
> How did the plan evolve over time?
> What can you learn from this game about communication and problem solving?

ASSET CATEGORIES Empowerment, Social Competencies

MISSION POSSIBLE

TIME 30–60 minutes

SUPPLIES
> Note cards
> Markers
> Two boundary markers (rope, tape, sticks)
> 10 flat items to stand on
   (carpet squares, boards, bathmats cut into squares, bases)

SET UP Place two boundary markers 20–30 feet apart in the playing area.

THE GAME Have players line up behind one of the boundary markers. Explain that "success in life" is found on the other side of the far boundary. The team's mission is to make sure that everyone succeeds in life (we are in this together, after all!). Between the beginning of life and success is the "stuff," warts and all. Have players write on note cards some of the stuff of their lives (the challenges, obstacles, distractions, and so on) that might get in the way of achieving success. It might be lack of focus, not enough time, or homework—write one obstacle per card.

Next, have players share what they have written. After all cards are read, have players place their cards in the "stuff" area. Players are not allowed to step on the "stuff" and must use their wits and resources to avoid it. Ask them to identify the resources they have going for them (teachers, each other, intelligence, parents, friends, and so on). You may need to ask players how they define "resources" first, and then ask them to give specific examples.

Tell them today they have 10 "resources" (flat items to step on) to help them get through "stuff" to "success" on the other side. Give the 10 items to the group and explain the following guidelines: As a group, they must deliver everyone to a successful life on the other side by touching only the 10 resources (no floor contact).

Players must stay in contact with the resources at all times. If one is not used, it is taken away. If someone accidentally touches the "stuff," the whole group must start again at the beginning. It is important to get as many of the resources to the other side as possible so that they can continue to be used after players reach "success." Ask if there are any questions, and then let players begin.

Once they've finished, have players count the number of resources they were able to keep. Play the game again, but this time ask them to set a goal for the number of resources they think they can retain.

GOING DEEPER

> What happened when you lost a resource?
> What resources do you most want to hang onto in life?
> Were you motivated by the knowledge that success was only 20–30 feet away?
> How do you stay motivated for "success" when you can't see it?
> Why do you think this activity focused on obtaining "success" for everyone?
> How does helping others succeed help you succeed, too?
> What "stuff" gets in the way of leading a healthy, successful life?
> What resources can you tap into to deal with that "stuff?"
> How did you learn from your mistakes in this group? At school? At home? In your faith community?
> What does it mean to take a trial-and-error approach to problem solving? What other approaches can you use?

ASSET CATEGORIES
Social Competencies, Support, Positive Identity, Boundaries and Expectations

TWO-SIDED TOSS

TIME 20–40 minutes

SUPPLIES
> Index cards (3–5 per player)
> Pens or pencils

THE GAME Start by asking the group to think about particular worries in their lives. Have players write a worry on one side of an index card. Tell players not to sign their name or write on the other side of the card. Gather everyone in a circle. Players toss their cares (cards) to the wind. Have players take turns picking up a few cards and reading the worries out loud. Without identifying the person who listed the topic, allow a few minutes for players to discuss each worry. Let them give their sage advice on letting go of or conquering the worry.

For the next round, ask everyone to find his or her original card. Tell them to think of a goal they have for their lives. (The flip side of worry is to focus energy on the positive, on an action they can do and work toward.) Have players write the goal on the blank side of their card. Gather in a circle again and have players toss their cards into the air. Players can pick a few cards at random and read the goals. Allow a few minutes to discuss each card and let them encourage each other to reach for their goals. Players should find their original cards and record any ideas, advice, or thoughts they want to remember.

GOING DEEPER

> How did it feel to name your worries and release them?
> Was there any advice that really struck you as wise or doable for any of the worries?
> Was it easy or hard to think of goals?
> What helps you focus on possibilities and move toward a positive future?
> Why is it important to set goals?
> What did you notice about the goals that were read? Are they big or small, short-term or long-term, involving one or more people?
> Do they involve learning something new (taking a new class, getting a job, learning a particular skill)?
> Would you like to set new goals as a result of this exercise?
> How can you support each other in your efforts to reach goals?

ASSET CATEGORIES
Social Competencies, Empowerment, Positive Identity, Commitment to Learning

HIDDEN HANDS

TIME 15–25 minutes

SUPPLIES
> Comic strip panels (one per group of 3–4 players)
> Envelopes (one per group)

SET UP Cut each comic strip into separate panels; place in envelopes.

THE GAME This activity gives participants practice in communicating with other team members and making group decisions. Instruct the participants to form groups of three to four members each. Distribute one envelope to each team. Direct members of each team to place the panels of the comic strip face down without examining them, and shuffle them around the table.

Members of each team should take turns selecting a panel (without showing it to the others) until all panels have been chosen. Team members describe their panels to the others, but are not allowed to see the other participants' panels or show their panels to others.

When team members agree upon the first panel in the cartoon (based on participants' descriptions), they place it face down on the table. After all the panels are face down in the order players have determined, they turn the panels over to see if the group has sequenced the comic strip in the proper order.

GOING DEEPER
> What communication process was used to describe the panels?
> What are the strengths and challenges of your communication style?
> How did the team decide the order for the panels?
> Did you readily share your opinions, or were you hesitant to share? Were you perhaps a bit too wordy in your sharing?
> How might this activity challenge your group to work more effectively together in the future?

ASSET CATEGORIES
Social Competencies, Commitment to Learning, Boundaries and Expectations

Stage 6

AFFIrmInG cHanGes anD ceLeBraTInG successes

This final stage deals with transitions and celebrations, natural occurrences within the life of any group or program. Although transitions and celebrations are the last stage of group development, building relationships never really ends. New situations call for ever-evolving connections. Programs end and members graduate, leave, or move away. You'll find rewarding ways to provide closure for changes, celebrate successes, and further connections with the games and activities in this section.

Celebrations are important—to individuals, groups, and program life cycles. Be intentional about using transitional activities and celebratory games to provide closure for a group's time together or to celebrate particular individual and group successes. When you build them into your program, you won't run short on time. If you mark important endings and departures within the group, members will come away from the experience feeling a real sense of affirmation and accomplishment.

Tips for Leading Transition and Celebration Games

These general questions can help you decide on an appropriate transitional or celebratory activity for your team:

- What is the end goal for our group's time together?

- Are there important life lessons, values, or special meanings that need to be captured through reflection?

- What is the mood of the team?
  Are members actively engaged or starting to disengage?
  Is the energy low and in need of picking up?
  Or does the group need a quiet moment to calm down?
  Do they need positive reinforcement? Recognition?

Depending upon your team's needs, choose the right activity to create unforgettable final moments. Consider these tips:

- Make it fun!

- Build on the final day's events
  (choose activities that tie in to what was being done).

- Remember—the "right" activity could be funny, reflective, affirming, ceremonial, a rite of passage, or full of simple laughter. There is no one right way!

IDEAS FOR CELEBRATIONS AND TRANSITIONS

Try these fun ideas for celebrating the successful conclusion of your group's time together. Enlist group members to help you personalize the final gathering.

- **Hold a pizza party or awards banquet** and put technology to work. Create slide show presentations with pictures and music, and showcase memories from the programming season.

- **Keep a scrapbook during the length of the program,** and pull it out at the end to reminisce about good times. Take lots of pictures, make copies, and dedicate a day to creating scrapbooks. People can write notes to each other to create lasting gifts for each other's scrapbooks.

- **When groups create team names, cheers, and songs, use them** at the end of meetings or activities to pump up the group and reinforce identity.

- **A team motto can be the rallying cry** at the beginning or ending of each gathering.

- **Print the team motto on t-shirts** at the end of the program season, and let everyone sign their names with permanent marker as a keepsake.

- **For a team awards banquet or ceremony, recognize members who are moving on or graduating.** Let members create fun awards categories in advance that include everyone in the group (Loudest Laugh, Tender Heart, Group Hugger, Peacekeeper, and so on). Awards can be made from inexpensive materials at an earlier meeting. Let everyone vote on the winners of each award. When you distribute awards, build suspense over the identity of each winner and tell a story or mention things you appreciate about each person. Tell how you've watched the person grow. This adds to the fun and makes each person feel special.

- **Let players create and perform dramatic skits** that reflect memories of their time in the program, and honor the various members who are leaving.

JUST FOR LAUGHS!

These debriefing questions can be used with any of the celebration and transition activities. Specific "Going Deeper" questions are provided with individual games when the game goes even further.

- What did you enjoy most today? Why?

- What concerns, if any, do you have about what you experienced today?

- What word (facial expression or body movement) would you use to describe your experience today?

- What was the most valuable part of being with the team today?

- What was the funniest moment?

- How did you contribute to making today's time together fun and valuable?

- What's one thing you learned today?

HULA HOOP CHALLENGE

TIME 20 minutes

SUPPLIES
> Two large hula hoops
> Stopwatch

THE GAME Ask the group to form a circle and hold hands, except for two players who each place a hula hoop over one arm and then clasp hands with their neighbors. See how quickly participants can pass the hoops around the circle (across arms and around bodies), sending hoops in opposite directions without breaking handclasps. Repeat several times.

GOING DEEPER
> What was the key to success in this activity?
> What did you learn as a team from this game about creative

problem solving? How have we exercised those skills through other group activities?

> How might you see this game as a metaphor for going in circles? Where do you spend your time going in circles?

> Were you skeptical at first about how to accomplish this task? How has this group moved from uncertainty to self-confidence in problem solving?

> How can planning help you manage your time wisely?

ASSET CATEGORIES   Social Competencies, Boundaries and Expectations

HA! HA!

TIME   10 minutes

THE GAME   Have one player lie down on his or her back. The next player lies down with her or his head on the first person's belly. Players continue lying down in this fashion until everyone is connected head to belly. Without laughing, the first player says "Ha!" the second, "Ha! Ha!" the third, "Ha! Ha! Ha!" and so on, adding one "Ha!" for each player. If someone laughs for real (and it's bound to happen), the group must restart the game with a new leader starting the laughter.

GOING DEEPER
> What makes you laugh?
> Why is laughter good for us?
> How can we laugh more each day?

ASSET CATEGORIES   Constructive Use of Time, Support, and good ole fun!

THE AHHH! GAME

TIME 10–20 minutes

THE GAME Gather the group into a circle, leaving some elbow room between players. Stand in the middle, randomly point at a player, and yell "Ahhh!" The designated player raises both hands over his head and yells back "Ahhh!" Players to either side of this player grab their heads, and say "Ahhh!" as they turn to players on either side of them. If someone says "Ahhh!" out of order, or messes up the game in some other way, they're out.

VARIATION Vary the sounds or motions. Point to someone and say "Fresh!" That person responds with "Cool!" as they run their hands across their forehead, and players to either side say "Ahhh!" as they zig-zag their index fingers in front of their bodies.

ASSET CATEGORIES Constructive Use of Time, Support

BALLOON LAUNCH

TIME 5–15 minutes

SUPPLIES
> Balloons in different colors
> Masking tape

SET UP Use masking tape to mark a starting line for the balloon launch.

THE GAME Break the group into smaller teams of 4–6 players and give each team member balloons of the same color. Each team has a different color. Ask players to blow up the balloons as big as possible and hold them without tying them off. Players from each team line up at the starting line. Tell players the goal is to see which team's balloons can travel the farthest distance from the starting line in the short-est amount of time. Give teams one minute to see how far they can advance their team's balloons.

On the count of three, the first player on each team releases his or her balloon. The second player on each team finds the first balloon and runs to that spot. He or she then releases the next balloon. The third player comes forward and play continues until all players have released balloons (or time is up). The winning team is the one whose balloons have gone the farthest distance from the starting point. Repeat as desired, varying the length of time for competition, or adding additional challenge by having team members walk backward to their launch site.

GOING DEEPER

> What methods did people use to make their balloons travel farther? How well did these methods work?
> What things do you do simply to have fun and laugh?
> In what ways does laughter and fun help you relieve everyday stress?
> Is there anything our group needs to "release" before we close?

ASSET CATEGORIES Constructive Use of Time, Support, fun!

COIN TOSS RELAY

TIME 20–25 minutes

SUPPLIES
> Masking tape
> Two coins

SET UP Mark two lines with tape at opposite ends of a play area.

THE GAME Divide players into two teams, each with a designated leader. Have them line up behind a line at one end of the playing area. Give each leader a coin and have them stand at the other end of the playing area across from their team. Each team leader flips a coin and calls out a task the next player in line must perform before running to join the leader across the opposite line. For instance, if heads, do 12 jumping jacks; if tails, whistle a tune. Substitute any fun action you prefer.

Players perform their task, run to their leader, stop and salute them, say their leader's name and repeat three times, "You're a valuable member of this team!" bow, and take the coin from the leader. They become the new leader. Play continues until all players have taken a turn. The first team to complete the relay wins. When both teams are finished, have each team turn and bow to the other.

GOING DEEPER

> Describe situations when you have been both a leader and a follower.
> Which is better—for a group to have one designated leader, or a system in which leadership rotates? Explain.
> In this game, you playfully affirmed each other. How often do you compliment others in the midst of everyday life?
> Why might it be important to compliment others in the midst of a team project rather than just once it's done?

ASSET CATEGORIES
Positive Identity, Positive Values, Empowerment, Social Competencies

"Puzzle Relay" makes a great transition from one gathering to the next if a topic isn't going to be completed in a single meeting. Remove some puzzle pieces so that no one puzzle can be completed. When all teams reach the point of being unable to complete their puzzles, gather them in a circle and debrief them. Segue to the next meeting by saying, "No team ended up with complete puzzles—there were missing pieces. Today we picked up some of the 'pieces' of how we're going to work together as a team, but our work isn't done. Next week, we'll complete the picture of where we're going as a group. Come prepared next time to complete the picture."

PUZZLE RELAY

TIME 10–20 minutes

SUPPLIES

> 24-piece puzzles (one per team)
> Tables
> Masking tape

SET UP   Place all pieces of each puzzle face down on the table near the box top so teams can see the image. Leave space between puzzles for elbow room. Mark a starting line across the room from the tables.

THE GAME   Divide players into teams of 4–10 players and have them line up at one end of a playing area behind the tape. At the signal, the first player in each team will run to the table, turn over all puzzle pieces in one puzzle, and join together two. After making the connection, the first player will run back and tag the next person in line. The next person will link another puzzle piece and return to tag the third person in line. Play continues until one team completes a puzzle and is declared the winner.

GOING DEEPER

> What pieces of our group's activities stand out to you?
> Are there any missing pieces to our group? Are there things we need to learn or do to make *our* puzzle more complete?
> What excites you about how our group can (or has) come together?
> What pieces do others contribute to the group? What piece do you offer?

ASSET CATEGORIES
Support, Empowerment, Positive Values, Social Competencies

POSITIVE VIBES JAM

TIME 30–60 minutes

SUPPLIES
> Paper and pencils (or pens)

NOTE The words group members choose to describe themselves in "Positive Vibes Jam" express their sense of personal power, giftedness, and identity.

THE GAME Distribute paper and pencils to each player and ask them to reflect on the following topics for 1–2 minutes. Tell them to write three words on paper about themselves:

> An adjective that describes me.
> A word that expresses a skill or talent or gift I bring to the group (or the world).
> A word that expresses a hope I have for the future.

Next, divide the group into triads. Allow 20 minutes for each triad to share their words with each other and to use all nine words to create a song, skit, poem, jingle, rap, or story. When time is up, have each triad perform their creative work. Applaud and acknowledge each person's creativity and gifts.

GOING DEEPER
> What did you learn about each other?
> What happens when a team celebrates its strengths?
> How can you tap into your gifts and personal power to make your community, school, and place of worship a better place?
> What are ways you might help others tap their gifts and strengths?
> What can you do to recognize and affirm strengths in others that they might not see in themselves?
> What impact could your positive peer influence have on others' sense of identity?

ASSET CATEGORIES
Positive Identity, Constructive Use of Time, Support, Boundaries and Expectation

PATS ON THE BACK

TIME 15–20 minutes

SUPPLIES
> Construction paper
> Fine-tip washable markers
> Masking tape

NOTE Use "Pats on the Back" with a group that has regularly spent a good amount of time together. This activity could be done over an extended period, honoring one person at each meeting.

THE GAME Ask each participant to tape a piece of construction paper to his or her upper back. Then tell them to mingle and write a positive affirmation on each person's paper. (They might write "Thank you for encouraging me," or "Thank you for always working so hard on our tasks," or "Thanks for taking time to get to know me.") Leaders should also participate in the exercise. Writers can choose whether to sign their names or give anonymous encouragement. When players have had a chance to write something for everyone else, ask players to fold their papers without looking at them and tuck them away to read later at a quiet moment.

ASSET CATEGORIES
Positive Identity, Support, Positive Values, Boundaries and Expectations

MUSICAL CHAIRS AFFIRMATIONS

TIME 10–20 minutes

SUPPLIES
> Chairs (one per participant)
> Music
> Tape or CD player
> Masking tape

THE GAME Have players sit on chairs. When the music starts, players rotate around the chairs and sit when the music stops. The two players who land on the seats marked by tape are to stand and name one thing they appreciated about the group, or one way they have felt especially supported by the group. After sharing, continue on, starting and stopping the music at will.

ASSET CATEGORIES
Positive Identity, Boundaries and Expectations, Positive Values, Support

MAIL CARRIERS

TIME 15–20 minutes

SUPPLIES
> Paper and pens

THE GAME Have the group sit in a circle, and invite each person to write a letter to the person on his or her right, expressing thoughts, feelings, and ideas related to your group, club meeting, or group project or about things you've learned. Tell them to deliver the letter to their neighbor, then silently read the letter that has been delivered to them. Take time to share thoughts aloud, or have another letter-writing session to respond to their neighbor's thoughts. Collect the letters to record your group expressions.

NOTE You can have group members create and decorate mailbags from brown lunch bags. Encourage everyone to write and deliver notes for the length of the group activity, throughout a retreat, or over the school year. Making this part of the group's practice when members enter a meeting is a great way to let them doodle and transition between activities.

ASSET CATEGORIES
Positive Values, Support, Social Competencies, Empowerment

PERSONAL KEYS PUZZLE

TIME 20 minutes

SUPPLIES
> Large piece of butcher paper cut into puzzle pieces (one piece per player)
> Markers
> Clear tape

THE GAME Give each player a puzzle piece. Ask players to write or draw the personal characteristics that they bring to the team. Tape the puzzle pieces together as each person shares some of their personal assets with the rest of the team. Celebrate the power of your team and the many things your collective strengths can accomplish. Post the completed puzzle in a visible location as a reminder that the group is more than the sum of its parts.

ASSET CATEGORIES Positive Identity, Empowerment, Constructive Use of Time

ON A THOUGHTFUL NOTE

MUSIC MAKERS

TIME 20 minutes

SUPPLIES
> A variety of sound-making objects

NOTE If sound-making objects are unavailable, ask players to make sounds with their hands, mouths, arms, and legs (slaps, snaps, whistles, hums, stomps).

THE GAME Pass out the objects and ask players to create rhythms that express their experience during their time together. Put the rhythms together to make a group composition. The "music" can be used to describe how members feel about the group in general, to reflect on a project well done, and so on. Use the concept of your choice for quick reflection and sharing.

GOING DEEPER
> How did you decide what rhythm to make for yourself?
> How did your group decide on the group composition?
> What rhythms would you like to play together in future projects?
> What can you do to work more enjoyably and effectively together in the future?

ASSET CATEGORIES Constructive Use of Time, Support, Social Competencies

GRAB BAG

TIME 20–30 minutes

SUPPLIES

> Miscellaneous items (such as bouncy balls, stuffed animals, buckets, measuring cups, markers, and modeling clay)

THE GAME Place random items in the middle of your group circle. Ask each person to think of an item that best describes one of the following:

> His or her contribution to the group (personality, talent, expertise)
> The group identity
> The work they did on a project and what they accomplished
> The values they see the group uphold

In turn, invite each team member to hold up "her" or "his" item and share with the group why they chose the item and how it best represents the question posed. Challenge players to listen closely to one another so they can celebrate and build upon one another's skills, talents, and insights. As each player shares, ask the group if anyone has additional comments that relate to what was said. You might ask if others can think of strengths or contributions that the member didn't mention or notice in her- or himself.

POSTCARD VARIATION Instead of objects, bring a variety of post-cards for players to choose from and ask them to explain their choice of card. "Our team is most like this postcard because . . . ." or "My contributions or my experience of the group is most like this postcard because . . . ."

ASSET CATEGORIES Support, Empowerment, Positive Values, Positive Identity

TALENT WEB

TIME 25–30 minutes

SUPPLIES
> Large ball of string or yarn
> Balloons
> List of questions (see "It's All in the Questions" on page 216)

THE GAME Ask the group to sit in a circle. Holding on to the end of a large ball of string, toss the ball across the circle to another team member (but not a next-door neighbor) after answering a question. (Many topics work; for instance, ask about players' individual needs, contributions to the group, or what individuals have learned today.) Players keep answering and tossing the string until everyone has had a chance to respond. Each player holds on to the string as they toss it to the next person. The circle will be connected by a web fashioned from the strengths and talents of every individual in the group. After admiring the web, throw balloons on top of the web to juggle together. Juggling the balloons reminds us that we're strongest when we all bring our talents, gifts and strengths to the group.

GOING DEEPER
> How have your differing characteristics and perspectives strengthened our team?
> Were you surprised to find that others have similar thoughts and feelings?
> In what ways do you bring 100 percent of your individual skills and talents to the group?

ASSET CATEGORIES
Support, Positive Values, Empowerment, Positive Identity, Social Competencies

SNAPSHOTS

TIME 20–25 minutes

THE GAME This activity is good for reflection after a group project or activity ends. Divide into small teams of 4–6 participants. Ask participants to use their bodies to pose as if for "snapshots" of scenes that represent different stages of the group's development (or the project that the group completed). Have players walk the group through their "photo album" of times they remember most, enjoyed the most, and learned from the most. Be sure to have one person describe the "snapshots" as the small group poses.

GOING DEEPER
> What stood out as each group went through the photo album?
> What memories were jogged for you?
> Why is it important to take time to remember?
> What can remembering tell us about our friendships and ourselves?

ASSET CATEGORIES Constructive Use of Time, Social Competencies, Support

OPPOSITE ENDS

TIME 20–25 minutes

SUPPLIES
> Masking tape
> List of word pairs

SET UP Mark the floor with one line of tape. Create a list of opposite words or phrase pairs. For instance:

> Comic book/horror book
> Work/fun
> Sitting/running
> Fast food/home-cooked meal
> Action movie/romantic comedy
> Spontaneous/ planned

> Day in the country/day in the big city

> Quiet, calm evening/big loud party

THE GAME Gather players around the center of the room and read aloud pairs of words or phrases. Tell the group to choose the phrase in each pair that best reflects their experience of time spent with the group. If they choose the first option, players move to the left end of the continuum (the line of tape). If they choose the second word, they'll move to the right end of the continuum. Call on a few volunteers after each word pair to explain why they're standing where they are.

GOING DEEPER

> Why do you think people can go through the same experience and have different reactions?

> What have we learned about ourselves as a group?

> How can we learn to accept differences in each other?

> What can we do to make our time together even better next time? More fun?

> What would help make it more meaningful?

ASSET CATEGORIES Empowerment, Positive Identity, Positive Values

BOX OF LIFE

TIME 10 minutes

SUPPLIES

> Paper and pencil (one per participant)
> Shoebox

THE GAME Hand out paper and pencils to all players. Note that during difficult times we sometimes use inspiring mottoes to help lift our spirits. Instruct each person to write an inspiring motto on a piece of paper. Tell them to try relating their motto to the theme of the meeting. (For example, for a seminar on time management or team building, you might write: "Don't put off until tomorrow what you can do today." For a motivational seminar, you might jot down "It's not the size of the dog in the fight, but also the size of the fight in the dog.")

Pass the box around the room, and ask each person to add his or her motto to it. Next, pass the box around the group and let players choose a new motto at random. Let them read the mottoes aloud and then place them back in the box. After the box returns to you, promise the group that you'll compile and send each of them the collected mottoes. You can be as simple or as creative as you like, typing mottoes onto a single sheet or collecting them into an elaborate scrapbook. This becomes a keepsake of what the group has learned from each other and of how they can remember each other.

GOING DEEPER

> Did you draw a quote or motto that felt like a message written especially for you?
> Of all the mottoes read, which ones really stood out? Why?
> Was there one motto read that seems to fit our group as a whole? If not, what should our group's motto be?
> How can quotes or sayings help inspire you to "stay the course" and keep trying?
> What is it about quotes that speak to something deep inside us?

ASSET CATEGORIES Support, Constructive Use of Time, Commitment to Learning, Positive Identity, Positive Values

TALKING STICK

TIME 3–4 minutes per player

SUPPLIES
> A stick
> Feather or ribbon
> Flute or drum music
> Nature poem

SET UP Tie a feather or ribbon to the stick. Have the group decorate the stick before forming a circle.

THE GAME Gather the group in a circle and let everyone center himself or herself quietly as they listen to the music. Read a poem relating the group's connection to the natural environment and to each other. Ask participants to come up with a single word that expresses the group's value, such as *trust, hope, openness,* or *care.* This "value" is the word that will be discussed by each member as they pass the talking stick from person to person. You may also pose a question for quiet reflection and response as the stick is passed. Each person is encouraged to hold the stick in silence for 1–2 minutes before speaking. Only the person holding the stick can speak, while everyone else remains silent and reflective, breathing quietly, listening. The person says what is on his or her heart and mind. After speaking, the member repeats the value word and passes the stick on. If he or she has nothing to say, the person simply speaks the value word aloud as he or she passes the stick to the next person. Everyone will have a second opportunity to speak.

GOING DEEPER
> What has being a part of this group meant to you?
> What will you always remember about your time in this group?
> How has our named value become meaningful to you?
> What have you learned from the group? How have you grown?

ASSET CATEGORIES
Positive Identity, Social Competencies, Positive Values, Support, Empowerment

Appendixes

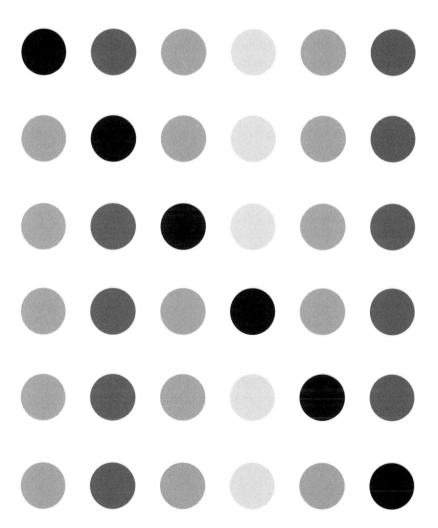

It's All in the Questions

Pull your favorite questions from this list for any of the games that need conversation starters. Add your favorite questions to the end of the list for future games.

- Who has traveled outside the country?
- Who is an oldest child? A youngest child?
- Who has lived in more than one city?
- Who has a close friend involved in a dangerous activity?
- Describe your cooking skills and your favorite thing to cook.

- Have you ever been camping? Tell about your experiences.
- Did you have a favorite subject in school? One you dreaded?
- Did you have a favorite T.V. or radio show as a child?
- Tell about one of your favorite books or magazines.
- Have you met or worked with any famous people?

- If you could live anywhere, where would it be? Why?
- Tell about any pets you had as a child.
- Tell about favorite games you played as a child.
- Are you responsible for household chores? What are they?
- What did you do as a child that got you into the most trouble with your parents? How did they handle it?

- Who has participated in a dangerous activity?
- Who sometimes feels unsafe at school?
- What instrument do you play or wish you could play?
- What is your full name? How did you get your name?
- What is the one invention you could not live without and why?

- What is your favorite Saturday activity?
- What is your advice to those younger than you?
- Do you prefer vanilla or chocolate?
- What is your ideal vacation?
- What is your favorite flavor of ice cream?

- Who helps you grow as a leader?
- Who cheers you on and listens to what you have to say?
- What is one thing you wish everyone knew about you?
- When you're in a new group, what do you do?

- What is one way you wish you could make the world a better place?
- Is there anything you've wanted to do but couldn't? What is it?
- What does giving to the community mean to you? What do you mean to the community?
- What is one thing you are really proud of in your life?
- If money were no object, what would you do?

- If time weren't an issue, what would you do?
- What would be the best birthday ever?
- What can you do to change the world for the better?
- What's one of your dreams?
- Does your community value young people? How?

- What makes you feel strong inside?
- What has been the most outstanding service project you've ever done? Why?
- How does it help you to help others?
- Do you try to do a good deed every day?
- In what ways are you a leader?

- How are you a role model for your friends and for people younger than you?
- What does it mean to have power over your life? How do you use your power for good?
- Is everyone creative, or are only some people creative?
- What are you interested in learning about?
- Is learning only important because it helps you get good grades?

- What do you care about?
- What is your favorite motto to live by?
- What do you think life is all about?
- Does equality mean everyone has to be the same?
- How can we be different and still respect one another?

- Are you brave enough and strong enough to tell the truth?
- How do you know when to speak out and when it's time to wait quietly?
- How do you know your life has a purpose?
- What will your future be like? What do you imagine?

- What does it mean to have personal power?
- Do you live each day with attention?
- If you could change one thing in the world, what would it be?
- If you could change one thing about your community, what would it be?
- If you could change one thing about people, what would it be?

- If you could do something for someone else without them knowing it was from you, what would you do?
- What day is your birthday and what year were you born?
- What city (ies) did you grow up in?
- What did you do for fun when you were young and what hobbies did you have?
- What is your favorite childhood memory?

- Who was your child hero?
- Did you have a favorite family vacation you took as a child?
- What is your favorite subject in school?
- Do you play sports or were you on any teams?
- What is your favorite season and why?

- What are the most important lessons your parents have taught you?
- Who is your favorite teacher and why?
- Who is your favorite leader and what qualities do they possess?
- What is your greatest concern about our world today?
- What is your favorite book? Movie? Why?

- What is your hope for the world?
- Who is your best friend and why?
- What helps you handle the hard parts of life?
- What gives you joy?

Game Index

You'll find all games in this book listed alphabetically below. The index summarizes key characteristics of games, such as suggested game locations (indoors and outdoors), relative physical and emotional risk levels, energy levels (quiet and active), and whether supplies are needed for each game.

GAME	PAGE	LOCATION		RISK LEVEL			ENERGY LEVEL		SUPPLIES
		INSIDE	OUTSIDE	LOW	MED	HIGH	SITTING	MOVING	
20 Words or Less	108	•	•	•			•		•
The Ahhh! Game	200	•	•		•			•	
Airplane Aerobics	71	•		•				•	•
Airplane Relay	88	•	•	•			•		•
All Aboard	181	•	•		•			•	•
Alphabet Race	109	•			•		•		•
Animal Corners	54	•	•	•			•		•
Artist of the Day	136	•		•			•		
Back-to-Back Art	139	•	•	•			•		•
Backward Lean	162	•	•			•	•		
Bag of Questions	56	•			•		•		•
Bag of Skits	132	•		•			•		•
Balloon Body Bop	99	•	•		•			•	•
Balloon Body Combo Bop	100	•	•		•			•	•
Balloon Bop	99	•	•		•			•	•
Balloon Chaos	100	•	•		•			•	•
Balloon Launch	200	•		•				•	•
Behind Every Name	26	•	•			•	•		
Big Issues Board Game	122	•		•			•		•
Blind Count	178	•	•	•			•		
Blind Design	136	•			•		•		
Blob Tag	85	•	•	•				•	
Bounce	67	•	•		•			•	
Bounce Machine	170	•	•			•		•	
Box of Life	213	•	•		•		•		•
Build a Boat	125	•		•			•		•
Building Blockbusters	123	•			•		•		•

GAME	PAGE	LOCATION		RISK LEVEL			ENERGY LEVEL		SUPPLIES
		INSIDE	OUTSIDE	LOW	MED	HIGH	SITTING	MOVING	
Bumpity, Bump Bump Bump!	25	•	•		•		•		
Card Castles	130	•		•			•		•
Cat and Dog Chase	84	•	•	•				•	
Change Over	181	•	•		•			•	•
The Chocolate Factory	182	•	•			•		•	•
Clay Artists	120	•		•			•		•
Clay Sculptures	128	•			•		•		•
Coin Toss Relay	201		•		•			•	•
Colorful Conversations	52	•	•		•			•	
Commercial Spots	134	•			•		•		•
Common Ground	60	•	•		•		•		•
Compass Lean	165	•	•			•	•		
Create-a-Game	121	•		•			•		•
Create a Message	133	•			•		•		•
Crossing the Line	152	•	•			•	•		
Crossword Connections	33	•	•	•			•		•
Dance Craze	70	•				•		•	
Debate a View	146	•			•		•		
Digital Scavenger Hunt	104	•	•	•				•	•
Diversegories	62	•		•			•		•
Diversity ABCs	64	•			•			•	•
Diversity Toss	92	•	•		•		•		•
Elbow Tag	87	•	•	•				•	•
Elevation	98	•	•		•			•	•
Expert Reviewers	114	•	•		•		•		
Family Chatter	57	•				•	•		•
Finger Fencing	68	•	•		•			•	
Fire in the Hole	101	•	•		•			•	•
Forward Lean	163	•	•			•	•		
Four Corners Dash	77	•	•	•				•	
Four Letter Words!	107	•			•			•	•
Four on a Couch	37	•			•		•		
Funny Bones	75	•	•		•			•	•

GAME	PAGE	LOCATION		RISK LEVEL			ENERGY LEVEL		SUPPLIES
		INSIDE	OUTSIDE	LOW	MED	HIGH	SITTING	MOVING	
Going for "It"	84	•	•		•			•	•
Grab Bag	209	•	•		•		•		•
Group Juggle	93	•	•	•				•	•
Group Poetry	112	•	•		•		•		•
Guiding Lights	184	•	•			•		•	•
Ha! Ha!	199	•				•	•		
Hidden Hands	194	•		•			•		•
Hog Call	47	•	•	•				•	
Hula Hoop Challenge	198	•	•		•			•	•
Human Machines	126	•	•		•			•	
Human Treasure Hunt	65	•	•	•				•	•
Ice Cream Sundae Challenge	179	•	•		•			•	•
Impulse	48	•	•	•			•		
In the Spotlight	36	•	•		•		•		•
"It" Tag	86	•	•	•				•	•
It's Your Birthday	24	•	•	•				•	•
Jungle Beat	79		•		•			•	•
Kitchen Creations	129	•		•			•		•
Last Detail	154	•	•		•			•	
Last One Standing	80	•	•		•			•	•
Leadership Line-Up	46	•	•	•				•	
Leaning Book Ends	164	•	•			•		•	
License Plates	38	•	•		•		•		•
Life Lines	151	•				•	•		•
Life Story	69	•	•		•			•	
Magical Stones	175	•				•		•	•
Mail Carriers	206	•			•		•		•
The Matching Game	34	•			•		•		•
Milling to Music	28	•			•		•		•
Mini-Scavenger Hunt	49	•	•	•			•		
Mission Possible	191	•	•			•	•		•

GAME	PAGE	LOCATION		RISK LEVEL			ENERGY LEVEL		SUPPLIES
		INSIDE	OUTSIDE	LOW	MED	HIGH	SITTING	MOVING	
Music Makers	208	•	•		•		•		•
Musical Chairs Affirmations	205	•			•			•	•
Mystery Partners	39	•			•		•		•
The Name Game	27	•	•	•			•		
Name Pulse	24	•	•	•			•		
Name That Tune	113	•	•	•			•		
Names in Action	22	•	•		•			•	
National Air Guitar	70	•	•		•			•	
Nature Sculptures	127	•	•		•		•		•
On Your Mark	91	•	•	•			•		•
One-Handed Shoe Tie	68	•	•		•			•	
Opposite Ends	211	•			•			•	•
Over and Under	89	•	•	•				•	•
Pan Game	57	•	•		•			•	•
Pantomime Pairs	135	•	•	•			•		
Parallel Words	110	•	•		•		•		
Pass the Can	82	•	•	•				•	•
Pats on the Back	205	•			•			•	•
Peek-a-Who?	38	•	•		•		•		•
Perfect Square	190	•	•		•		•		•
Personal Keys Puzzle	207	•			•		•		•
Personality Sketches	54	•		•			•		•
Picture Perfect	119	•		•			•		•
Player to Player	75	•	•	•				•	
Popcorn	97	•	•	•			•		•
Positive Vibes Jam	204	•	•		•		•		•
Precious Treasure	96	•	•		•		•	•	•
Predators and Prey in the City	83	•	•	•				•	
Puzzle Relay	202	•			•			•	•
Quick Scavenger Hunt	102	•	•	•				•	•

GAME	PAGE	LOCATION		RISK LEVEL			ENERGY LEVEL		SUPPLIES
		INSIDE	OUTSIDE	LOW	MED	HIGH	SITTING	MOVING	
Raise the Bar	78	•	•		•			•	•
Scatter Categories	124	•	•	•				•	
Share and Tell	29	•	•		•		•		•
Sherpa Walk	172	•	•			•		•	•
Shrinking Ship	81	•	•		•			•	•
Signal Switch	69	•	•		•			•	
Silent Scramble	25	•	•	•			•		
Singing Names	21	•	•		•		•		
Sit Down, Stand Up	67	•	•		•			•	
Slap, Clap, Snap!	22	•	•			•	•		
The Smiling Game	50	•	•	•			•		
Snapshots	211	•	•		•			•	
Snowshoes	180	•	•		•			•	•
Song Off	131	•			•		•		•
Speed Rabbit	90	•	•		•			•	
Spell Off	106	•			•			•	•
Sticky Buns	156	•			•			•	•
Sticky IDs	32	•	•		•		•		
Story Circles	111	•	•		•		•		
Take a Hike	35	•	•		•			•	•
Take a Stand	143	•			•		•		•
Talent Web	210	•	•		•		•		•
Talking Points	68	•	•		•			•	
Talking Stick	214		•		•		•		•
Tandem Stand Up	171	•	•		•			•	
Team Banners	31	•	•	•			•		•
That's Me!	30	•	•		•			•	•
Ticket Talk	58	•	•		•		•		•
Tiny Teach	61	•	•		•			•	
Toss-a-Name	23	•	•		•			•	•
Trivia Acts	118	•	•	•				•	•
Trivia Masters	117	•	•		•		•		•
Trust Fall	169	•	•			•		•	
Trust Lift	167	•	•			•		•	
Trust Walk	168	•	•			•		•	

GAME	PAGE	LOCATION		RISK LEVEL			ENERGY LEVEL		SUPPLIES
		INSIDE	OUTSIDE	LOW	MED	HIGH	SITTING	MOVING	
TV Families	116	•	•	•			•		•
Two Circles	149	•	•		•		•		
Two-Sided Toss	192	•				•	•		•
Two Truths and a Lie	59	•	•		•		•		•
Unfair Quiz Show	114	•	•	•			•		
Values Continuum	147	•	•			•	•		
What Would You Do If...?	144	•	•		•		•		
Who Am I?	137	•			•		•		•
Who's the Leader?	44	•	•	•			•		
Wind in the Willows	166	•	•			•	•		
The Winding Road	185	•	•			•		•	•
The Winding Road: Crossing the Pit of Despair	187	•	•			•		•	•
The Winding Road: Crossing the Sea of Hope	188	•	•			•		•	•
Wink, Wink!	155	•	•		•			•	
You Belong!	48	•	•	•				•	
You're a Star!	45	•	•		•			•	•
Zip!	94	•	•	•				•	•
Zip Bong	43	•	•	•			•		
Zoom	43	•	•	•			•		

Game Sources

Funn 'N Games by Karl Rohnke. Dubuque, IA: Kendall/Hunt Publishing Co., 2004.

A Compact Encyclopedia of Games, Games, Games for People of All Ages compiled by Mary Hohenstein. Minneapolis, MN: Bethany House Publishers, Inc., 1980.

Inspired to Action: A Leadership Activities Guide for Groups Working for the Common Good by David Kelly-Hedrick. Available at dkhedrick@mc.seattleymca.org.

Learning on the Run: Active Christian Learning Experiences for Youth and Adults by Ted Endacott. Nashville, TN: Discipleship Resources, 2005.

QuickSilver: Adventure Games, Initiative Problems, Trust Activities, and a Guide to Effective Leadership by Karl Rohnke and Steve Butler (Project Adventure, Inc.). Dubuque, IA: Kendall/Hunt Publishing Co., 1989.

Silver Bullets: A Guide to Initiative Problems, Adventure Games and Trust Activities by Karl Rohnke (Project Adventure, Inc.). Dubuque, IA: Kendall/Hunt Publishing Co., 1984.

Youth Leadership in Action: A Guide to Cooperative Games and Activities Written by and for Youth Leaders (Project Adventure, Inc.). Dubuque, IA: Kendall/Hunt Publishing Co., 1995.

About the Authors

SUSAN RAGSDALE cofounded and directs the Center for Asset Development. She works as a trainer, consultant, and writer. Susan has more than 15 years' experience in the youth and community development field with the YMCA of Middle Tennessee, where she's been involved with a variety of programs ranging from inner-city sports to environmental service-learning.

Susan's fondness for using games to actively engage others begins with memories of her third- and fourth-grade teachers (thanks, Ms. Colleen and Mrs. Martin), who made learning fun by playing "Spelling Baseball" and "History Jeopardy." As a 14-year-old summer sports camp counselor, she created wacky games to keep the campers—only two years younger!—moving and having a good time. Susan discovered that games were a fun way to explore life lessons and she's been using games to build groups ever since. Susan lives in Nashville, Tennessee, with her husband, Pete, and their two dogs.

ANN SAYLOR is a trainer, author, and cofounder of the Center for Asset Development. She has written more than 100 articles in the areas of youth leadership, service-learning, character development, personal balance, and youth and adult partnerships. One of the first workshops Ann led was "Playing Games—Not Just Fooling Around" with Cynthia Scherer of Points of Light Foundation.

Ann's fascination with games began when she looked for new ways to teach teenagers in classrooms, camps, and conferences. Realizing most people (herself included) learn more effectively when they're active, experimenting with new behaviors, and solving challenges, she found games to be the answer and started collecting them from colleagues and friends. Ann describes herself as a dreamer and connector, always looking for ways to help people, schools, teams, and organizations function their best. She loves to laugh and enjoy life to the fullest! Ann lives in Pleasant View, Tennessee, with her husband, Dan, and three children.

Susan and Ann invite you to send your favorite games, tips, and ideas to their Center for Asset Development web site, info@theassetedge.net.

Game Leader Notes

Add your favorite games, notes, ideas, and additional discussion questions here.

Game Leader Notes